BORN TO BE WILD

By K.J. Houtman

Minneapolis, Minnesota

This book is dedicated to Skyler Houtman, born on 9/11 and currently serving a tour of duty in Afghanistan with the U.S. Army as a Cavalry Scout. Thank you for your service to our country, son. *Very* proud of you, *and* very proud and thankful to all those who serve in the military and their families. God bless the U.S.A. and the freedoms we enjoy.

Copyright © 2012 by K.J. Houtman
Cover design by Scott Milawski with copyright © by Fish On Kids Books LLC. All rights reserved. No part of this book may be reproduced, stored in a retrieval system or transmitted in any way (photocopying, recording, electronic transfer or otherwise) without the prior written permission from Fish On Kids Books LLC, except for the inclusion of brief quotes for a review or marketing effort.

Fish On Kids Books LLC
P.O. Box 3
Crystal Bay, MN 55323-0003
Website address: www.fishonkidsbooks.com

Library of Congress Control Number: 2012950785
ISBN: 9780982876084

Other works by K.J. Houtman

A Whirlwind Opener
Driving Me Crazy
Spare the Rod
Duck, Duck Deuce

FIRST EDITION 2012
Manufactured in the United States of America

Chapter 1

"Deep fried gopher guts'd sell here," Pops harrumphs from a few steps behind the rest of the family. He reaches up to touch his right temple, massaging just above his eye.

Just days away from turning 12, Gus Roberts is spending the last day of summer vacation at the Minnesota Great Get-Together—the State Fair. For Gus' family: parents Annie and Jim, 16-year-old brother Jake, and grandfather Hessel Riss—everyone calls him Pops—the fair is a summer ritual more about food than anything else.

"Dipped in chocolate," Annie replies, as she stops for a moment to wait on the old guy. They don't look related at all. Pops is a big man with white, wispy hair. Annie's petite with long, black, shiny hair. She was adopted from Korea as a baby.

"On a stick, Mom. Has to be on a stick," Gus adds as the whole family chuckles. Jim and Jake grab from a small white bag of mini donuts. Gus offers one to his mom. Annie shakes her head in reply and Gus pops the whole thing in his mouth, and licks the sweet coating from his sticky digits.

"Okay, we're at our favorite spot for cheese curds and garlic fries," Jim stops the group on the corner.

"I don't have any more room." Annie places a hand on her protruding belly. With her third child due next month, she's not walking too fast either.

"There's always room for cheese curds, Mom."

"And milk," Gus adds. "We need some Sweet Martha's chocolate chip cookies and all-the-milk-you-can-drink for a dollar."

"Oh, you guys," Annie replies. "I'll get the cheese curds inside the building. You order the fries." She gestures to a small line near the sports pavilion. "And check on the score for me while you're there."

Big TVs face the center court of the sports pavilion and everyone is watching the Minnesota Twins. They are playing the Chicago White Sox in an afternoon match up today—Labor Day. It's getting tense heading into the end of the season with play offs around the corner. Annie works for the Twins as the director of public relations. Luckily, she didn't need to travel to Chicago for an away series this weekend. Then again, it's getting kind of hard for her to travel. Gus' baby sister is due in just a little over a month.

The guys inch forward in the line, with one eye on the monitors. The game is tied up, one all, bottom of the sixth.

"One large garlic fries," Jim orders as they reach the counter. In a moment, the aromatic treat is in his hands and the boys are quick with a preliminary snitch, as Jim drenches a corner with ketchup.

Gus looks around. He sees Pops standing in front of the TV monitor; more interested in the game than the next round of State Fair treats. Pops is a tough, old naval aviator and a big baseball fan.

"Dad, I'm going to pay for this when wrestling practice starts this fall," Jake mumbles, as a handful of fries with fresh minced garlic enters his mouth.

"You'll be fine. When does practice start?" Dad asks. School year starts tomorrow.

"Captains' practice? October. Officially with the coach, November," Jake answers with a mouthful. "You know I'm always training, Dad."

"I know and it pays off, son. Everyone will be gunning to beat you this year. You're a reigning State Champ now." Jim stands tall as he says it and pats Jake on the shoulder. "Kudos to them if they can pin you, or even win a decision against you."

"I guess so. Have to keep my A game going." Jake smiles. "Hope to hit 200 wins."

"That's a good goal, Jake," Jim replies. "Hard to reach—but a good one."

"You should go out for wrestling, Gus," Jake offers his little brother. The two boys look a lot alike with warm cinnamon skin and black, shiny hair like their mother. They get long legs and height from their father. The four years in age is less noticeable this summer. Gus has been growing like a weed lately.

Gus shrugs, feeling the pressure of Jake's accomplishments. "Dad and I have a fishing tournament coming up. Right Dad?" Gus has been researching the little walleye factory in South Dakota where the tournament will be—Lake Waubay. He's been studying topical maps and satellite screen shots, reading about past tournaments and the tecchniques that produced wins. He's been practicing with bottom bouncers so much on Lake Minnetonka over last few weeks that his hands are cut and scraped from all the fish he's handled.

"Do you have your half of the entry fee and expenses, Gus?"

"Yup, it's in the bank." All the days doing yard work at the neighbor's house over the summer has paid off. So has getting a sponsorship from St. Croix Rods to be on their pro-staff. He may only be a sixth grader, but this almost 12-year-old has his eye on the prize of professional angler. When the folks at St. Croix Rods found out about his dreams, they decided to help with sponsorship money. Kind of nice that someone thinks he has the potential.

"Once we pay for our entry fee, we can't get it back," Jim mentions, a good fisherman in his own right. Jim's a professional photographer and most of his clients are in the hunting and fishing business. He sometimes guides a little bit on the side, too. "Tournament fees are non-refundable so we have to be sure." The guys watch Annie waddle towards them with the red and white paper boat of greasy goodies.

"I'm 'in like Flynn' as Pops would say. Right, Pops?" Gus looks over at his crusty old grandfather who has his own way of turning a phrase. Pops moved in with the family when his wife died, Annie's adopted mom. That was just about the time Gus was born. Right now, Pops is looking down at the ground and has two fingers pressed firmly against the center of his forehead.

Annie returns and hands the hot treats to Gus and exhales. "Here, you take these," as she looks down to see the paper lining already littered with grease droplets. "I can't eat one more fried anything."

"I heard there's chocolate covered bacon on a stick here this year." Gus digs in and walks towards Pops "Sounds a little gross. But hey, everything's better with bacon, right?" Gus offers the tasty, melted-cheese treat, a staple of the State Fair experience.

Pops looks back at Gus, but doesn't respond. One eye seems to focus, but the other looks sleepy—or glassy. Pops attempts to reach up for a cheese curd, but try as he might, he can't get his arm to cooperate. It jerks and moves only an inch or two.

"Wha-aaa…" Pops mumbles, his voice thick and low. Sounds like he has a mouthful of oatmeal.

Gus has seen Pops like this before.

"Mom, something's wrong with…" Gus starts to tell his mother, but he doesn't get to finish. "POPS," he calls out frantically. Gus tries to catch the big man as he falls, dropping the cheese curds into the trampled grass. Pops is too big to catch. "HELP," Gus shouts to the family as he's down next to his grandfather.

"Oh my! Jim, call nine-one-one," Annie orders. Hard as it is to stoop down, she does, cradling the old man's head on her knees. She strokes the fine, white hair away from his eyes, speaking softly. "Pops, are you okay?"

Jim crouches down, low to the ground, and pulls the cell phone from his pocket. A crowd begins to form all around them. "Hang in there, Pops. We'll get you help."

"Nine-one-one emergency response," the female operator's voice comes through Jim's cell phone, set on hands free. "What is your emergency?"

"We're at the State Fair and my father-in-law just collapsed."

"We'll send help right away. Where are you, sir?" dispatch asks.

"At the sports pavilion, by the garlic fries vendor," Jim answers.

"Okay, what happened?"

"He just collapsed," Jim stammers. "I don't know what's wrong."

Gus was with Pops on the fishing opener in the spring. "It's a stroke, ma'am," Gus answers, loud enough for the hands-free speaker. His eyes shift from the cell phone and lock with his mother's. It's been the niggling worry in the back of both their minds for months. The risk so great after the earlier incidents. "My grandfather just had a stroke."

Chapter 2

"I'm a doctor," the man says as he bends down next to Annie. He looks about 30 years old and is wearing a Life is Good t-shirt, khaki shorts and flip flops. "Mind if I look?"

"No, please do," Annie replies, her breath is short and voice a little shaky.

The doctor checks Pops' pulse and looks at his eyes. "Did I hear you call the paramedics?" he asks Jim.

"Yes, I did. They should be here any second since they keep response teams stationed at the State Fair."

"That's good," the doctor adds as he continues his examination. "Did I hear someone say he's had a stroke? I was standing right beside you."

"Yes, that's what Gus said." Annie gestures to her sixth-grade son.

The doc looks at the boy with fishing lures on his t-shirt, well-groomed black hair tucked under a Ranger Boats cap, teeth straight and white.

"Maybe, if we're lucky, only a T.I.A," Gus adds.

The doctor stops what he's doing for a moment and looks more closely at Gus, sees his Asian eyes and high cheekbones. "What makes you think it is a Transient Ischemic Attack?"

"He's had two this year. One in March and a second in May," Gus replies. "I was with him during the second one and I had to take care of him. By myself. It was 14 hours before medical help arrived."

The sound of the siren arrives before the ambulance. In a moment, the paramedics push their way through the crowd with their equipment. The doctor takes charge.

"Take him to the University of Minnesota Hospital," the doctor instructs, and adds a few instructions on what to do enroute. "Preliminary indicators are a stroke. I want a CT scan of the brain as soon as he's stable."

The paramedics nod. One is starting an I.V. and the other is laying out the transport board.

"Is he on any medications?"

Annie rattles off the meds that Pops takes.

"I'll head over to the hospital and follow up. Do you want to ride in the ambulance or drive over?" the doctor asks.

"I'll ride." Annie tries to stand up, but needs help.

"I don't want to leave you. I'll ride along," Jim adds. "Jake, bring Gus in the truck and meet us at the hospital." He tosses the keys.

"Okay, Dad," Jake replies as he catches them.

Jim holds Annie's hand as he helps her step up into the back of the ambulance. The doors close and the *woop-woop-woop* of the ambulance opens up a path for departure through the people.

For a moment the boys' shoes are filled with lead and neither moves, although the crowd that gathered around them now disperses. They watch the vehicle meander through the crowded street, red and blue lights flashing. Siren on, as needed, to clear a path. Eventually, they can't see it anymore and they turn to look at each other.

"You know the way to the U of M hospital?" Jake asks.

"No."

Jake lets out a big sigh.

"But I can plug it into the nav unit in the truck," Gus adds. When it comes to electronics with GPS and sonar, like the fancy equipment in the family's Ranger boat, Gus is dialed in.

"Good."

Silence amongst a crowd of thousands. Check that. Hundreds of thousands.

"He didn't regain consciousness." Gus wrings his hands together, his eyes cast down on the ground. Memories flash by: making lunches, after school snacks, flying in Pops' plane, times they were fishing together. Times they didn't see eye to eye or get along, too.

"I know, Gus."

"Guess we should go." The lead in their shoes remains as they walk to the parking lot, the fun sites and smells of the fair melting away like a dropped ice cream cone on hot asphalt. Worried? Yes. In a hurry to find out the news? No. Navigating the crazy, busy streets and sidewalks of the State Fair, not having paid attention to where your dad parked the truck? A bit overwhelming.

As they pass the booth with the ritual of all-the-milk-you-can-drink for a dollar, Jake turns to his brother. "You still want some milk?"

Gus looks up at the lines around the vendor. "I think I'd puke."

"Yeah." They keep walking.

"Pops always said he had a 'rumbly in the tumbly' on the way to the parking lot when we'd leave." Gus' words dissolve in the light breeze as the boys merge into the swinging security circle-gate that doesn't allow re-admission, or a chance to sneak into the fair without paying the entrance fee.

"I sure hope he's okay. What would we do without him?" Jake asks.

Gus nods his head, remembering all the times Pops would brag about Jake's wrestling. So proud, he never missed any of Jake's matches and sometimes even watched practices. Pops, an avid hunter and a fisherman, was quiet on praise for big fish or big bucks. Only once had Gus ever heard 'good job' with regards to catching fish or a well-placed grouping during archery practice.

Will Pops get to watch his favorite grandson wrestle again? Will he ever do those outdoor things that he loves? Or fly his airplane that's been sitting since May, waiting for him to get better?

Gus swallows hard. "I don't like the feeling in my stomach this time, either."

Chapter 3

"Ooooh!" Annie shouts and doubles over. "Oh my!"

The boys are just approaching in the hospital hallway. They see her bent over, Jim holding on gently. They hurry the last twenty feet.

"You okay, Mom?" Jake asks. "Dad, what's going on?"

Jim rubs Annie's back. "Well…we've been waiting for word on Pops. I'm afraid some labor pains are kicking in for your mom."

"Labor pains?" Gus asks. "You're going to have the baby now?" His voice squeeks and he looks over at Jake. Both are a new shade of pale.

Annie straightens up and takes a deep breath. "I thought it was false labor. It can happen. But now I'm not so sure."

"Do you want to sit down? Let's go over to the chairs," Jim offers.

"I think you should go see a doctor," Gus adds.

"That's what I said. Honey, let's see if we can have a nurse or doctor talk with you. Maybe rest a little bit."

"Well, okay," Annie replies, breathing hard. "It would feel really good to lie down for a minute."

"We'll stay here, and come find you if we hear anything," Jake adds.

"Use this." Gus returns with a wheelchair that was abandoned in the hallway. "Seriously, Mom. Just take it easy and go talk to the nurses."

Annie leaves in the chair-on-wheels with Jim steering.

Jake and Gus settle in to the waiting area. They wait and wait.

And wait.

Eventually, Jake tosses down the last magazine and offers, "I think we've been forgotten."

After quite a long time, their dad walks in. "Hey."
"Hey yourself," Jake replies. "Finally. What's up?"
"Yeah, how's Mom?"
"She's resting," Jim replies. "But across the river at the Children's hospital. The doctors admitted her and started a medication to slow things down. With rest, they're hoping to postpone labor. Ideally, the baby will have more time, but if not they have a NICU there for preemies."
"What's a nick-you?" Jake asks.
"I.C.U. is Intensive Care Unit," the younger brother replies. "And Neonatal is…well, newborn babies."
Jake and his father exchange a look. "Brainiac," the older sibling murmurs.
All three guys sigh.
"Any news on Pops?" Gus asks.
"He's in surgery."
"What? We've been sitting right here. No one said anything."
"I'm sorry," Dad replies. "I'm running between two buildings here." Jim runs his hand through his hair. "They needed your mom to sign the papers to put in a stent or two. That's why I came over to get you."
"So he just went in?"
"Uh-huh," Jim mumbles. "Come on. I'll show you where the other building is." And they all traipse off together.

"Wow. All the men in the my life." Annie sounds a little melancholy as the guys walk into her room.
"All but one," Gus replies.
"I know buddy. I'm worried about him, too."
"I told the boys that Pops is in surgery. They wanted to see you and wait here for news."
"That's sweet. But really guys, I think you should head home. There's nothing you can do here and school starts tomorrow. It's getting late and Quick needs to be fed and let outside."

The boys exchange a look. No one likes getting dismissed, especially not for school starting back up. But someone does need to take care of their old yellow Labrador retriever.

"I'll rest better, and your dad can just focus on what's going on here," she adds. "It'll help if we know you're taking care of Quick and on track for school. We'll call you in the morning with news."

"In the morning?" Gus asks. "What about Pops?"

"Or sooner if there's news," Dad explains. "And this stent surgery is fairly routine. Come on, I'll walk you out to the truck."

As they travel the hallways and elevators to the parking ramp, Jim lets Jake get just a little bit ahead of their pace.

"Gus?" Jim says, quietly.

"Yeah, Dad?"

"With all that's going on, I don't see how we can head out to Waubay Lake on Friday night and pre-fish for the tournament." Jim and Gus' first professional fishing tournament together, slated for Webster, South Dakota. Gus' birthday weekend was for practice time on the water. Then the actual tournament would be the following weekend when he's 12 and within the rules for a professional-level tournament. Something he's been dreaming about for a long time and preparing for all summer.

"I-I suppose," Gus stammers.

"I know it's your birthday this weekend and we had it planned."

"I don't care about my birthday, Dad. That part doesn't matter." He doesn't tell him how much the other part does.

"I know. You have the worst birthday."

Gus swallows. There it is. He always thought so, but no one ever came right out and said it. Some people look so forward to their birthday. Not him. Except this year. It was actually going to be fun—or so he thought. "Maybe we can see how things go this week and figure it out later. It's only Monday. We were going to go on Friday after school."

"I know. But…" Jim pauses. "I won't be sending in the registration for the tournament tomorrow."

Gus stops walking for a second, then gets back in the groove. He doesn't say anything.

"Everything's just crazy right now. Listen, we'll talk more tomorrow. Right now my focus is your mom and Pops." Jim opens the side door for Gus.

"You boys okay getting up and out for school on your own?"

"Sure, Dad," Jake answers. "No problem. Can I take this or Mom's car to school?"

"No, take the bus. Both of you."

"Dad, I have to work at Rockvam after school tomorrow." Jake closes the door on the driver's side but opens the window.

"Ride your bike or take the boat or WaveRunner over for work." Jim knows that Jake can easily drive one of the watercraft to a marina.

Jake doesn't say anything. Gus doesn't either. Silence hangs in the air.

"Thanks for being understanding guys," Dad adds. "I'll text an update to your cell phone, Jake. You can let Gus know what's going on. Okay?"

Jake nods.

"Drive safely." Jim waves as Jake pulls out of the parking lot with his younger brother riding shotgun.

Not much is said on the half-hour ride back to Lake Minnetonka. The boys are thinking about, and praying for, two important people in their lives, suddenly both in the hospital. Everything in their own schedules is now topsy turvy. Neither boy saw it coming when the day began.

13

Chapter 4

Gus wakes up with Quick on the bed with him. "Come on Quickers, let's get you some kibble." At that the old Lab shakes off stiff joints and hops off the bed.

There's a note on the kitchen table:

> *Dad texted that Pops came through surgery just fine. They put in two stents. He was in recovery last I heard. Mom's still having labor pains, but fewer and not as close together. The docs want her to stay. That's all I know so far.*

Gus puts the note back down and grabs the stainless steel bowl and heads to the basement for Quick's kibble. The dog waits at the top of the stairs. Until last year he'd follow. These days his arthritis makes it hard for him to get around. Gus pours some milk over his cereal. Both boy and dog eat their nourishment in the kitchen and then Gus puts Quick outside for his morning business. He fills a spoon with peanut butter and adds two Glucosamine tablets. Quick gets the treat when he comes back inside. What the dog doesn't understand is how much the meds help him with his stiff joints. Soon, Gus is hurrying up to catch bus route 101.

The first day of sixth grade. It definitely feels different already. As soon as his friends Katie and Marsha board at their stop, he realizes why. They are the oldest ones on the bus. First time that's ever happened.

"Hi, Gus," Katie greets her friend, and she and Marsha sit down in front of Gus. She turns backwards. "You ready for another school year?"

"I guess."

"What's the matter, Gus?" Katie asks. "You sound kind of…sad."

"Oh…well," Gus stammers, unsure how much to share. "You know…"

"I know what you mean," Marsha interjects. "Summer vacation is always too short." She sighs. "Back to school. Bummer."

Gus nods. But Katie catches his eye and looks hard at him. Then she turns back around and chats with Marsha the rest of the way to school.

"Hey, Gus," Doogie calls as they walk into the building. "Man, we nailed 'em on Forrest Lake Bay yesterday."

"Nice size walleyes, Gus," Asher adds. Doogie and Asher are best friends, and sometimes Gus makes three. The trio walks in together, with Doogie and Asher doing most of the chatting about their time together over the last few days. The boys have been fishing hard—and often together. Gus has the scabs on his right hand to prove it. Fisherman's honor. Fisherman's hands.

Once inside, Katie turns to Gus since their lockers are so close together. "What's really going on?" Katie asks quietly, as she reads from a slip of paper with her locker number and code. She works on the new routine.

"What do you mean?" Gus has the new code to his locker memorized. They're only a couple apart and no one is standing in between them at the moment.

"I know you, Cornelius Gustav Roberts," Katie answers, even more quietly. "And something is wrong."

Gus bristles at the use of his full name. He looks over his shoulder to see if any of the older kids have heard. Then he remembers: they're the oldest this year. Gus sighs. His name is kind of a sore subject. He prefers simply Gus, and worries who will find out. Kind of embarrassing, and he hasn't told Doogie and Asher. His school records say C. Gustav Roberts. The guys have specifically asked what the C stands for and he still hasn't told them. Katie just asked Pops one day—and he blurted it out! Gus had to make her promise not to tell anyone.

The first bell sounds, as Katie hurries to class she calls over her shoulder, whipping her long strawberry-blonde pony tail around. "Later."

The bus after school is hectic, and Katie isn't on it. When Gus walks from the bus stop to his house, he sees Uncle Zach in the driveway.

"Hey," Gus calls to his favorite uncle—Jim's younger brother. Earlier this summer Zach and Riley got married. There were a few adventures around that whole event.

"Hey yourself," Zach holds the truck door open, delaying getting in as Gus approaches.

"What're you doing here, Zach?"

"Gave your dad a ride home from the hospital."

"I'm glad they're home."

"Not they. Just he. Your mom needs some things and when my bro calls, I'm on it. You'll have to get the DL from him." Zach jumps in the truck and closes the car door, window open. "Peace out." He flashes a deuce sign.

"Bye." Gus walks to the house and calls out over the music. "Dad?"

"Upstairs. Bedroom." A voice drifts down the stairs.

Gus runs up, two at a time to the beat of some rock 'n roll oldies playing on Pandora. "What's the update? How's everybody doing?"

"Surgery went well for Pops. He was so groggy afterwards, we didn't talk with him. Just the doctor."

"Two stents? Jake left me a note this morning."

"Yeah, hopefully it will help. But it wasn't a T.I.A. this time. It was the real deal. A stroke."

"I was worried that it was. What about Mom?"

"They slowed things down, but we're not out of the woods yet. Doctor wants her there to observe and monitor. When she does come home, probably bed rest until the baby is born."

"Wow. Hard for her to stay in bed all day."

"I know. Your mother is a go-getter," Jim replies. "But she'll do what she needs to do for the sake of the baby. A couple of more weeks will help a lot. Every day helps her be just a little bit bigger and her lungs a little bit stronger."

Her. The baby sister, yet to be born, needs a little more time.

"And it means we have to do what we can around here. Laundry, vacuuming, picking up—stuff like that." Jim finishes putting the last few things in a small suitcase and zips it shut.

"Sure, Dad."

"Jake's at work. He took the boat, he just left." Using the remote control to the wireless sound system, Jim turns down the volume on the tunes. His voice changes to a serious tone on his number two son, as he pats the top of the king-size bed. "Have a seat a second."

Gus hops on, but doesn't say anything. Jim sits down on the edge.

"I'm sorry about this weekend, not being able to pre-fish for our walleye tournament in South Dakota."

"I know, Dad. It's okay, I'm still gonna be ready. I've been doing a ton of research online. Looking at aerial photos and maps. Reading blogs from guides and tournament anglers. I've got a great game plan, so even if we don't get out early..."

Jim seems to struggle with the words, and stammers a bit. "I-I don't think we're going to be able to do this tournament at all, buddy. I don't see how we can with everything that's going on."

Gus' eyes open wide. "I thought you were just talking about missing this weekend pre-fishing. Not go at all? Cancel? All my planning, Dad. I've been working all summer to save up money for this." Gus' voice cracks just a little.

"I know you have, and I'm proud of you for that. I'm sorry."

"And I got the money from St. Croix Rods. It's supposed to help with entry fees."

"I know that too," Jim replies. "Think about it, though. How can we, really? With Pops having a stroke and the baby possibly coming early? And Mom on bed rest even if the baby goes full term. How could we go so far away?" It's a solid five-hour drive from Lake Minnetonka to Waubay.

He has a point. A huge point.

"Man..." There's a catch in Gus' voice. He looks away.

Jim rubs Gus' shoulder. "I know buddy. It stinks. It really stinks. I was looking forward to doing this together, too."

Gus looks up, startled at the lump in his throat. He pushes it down and takes a deep breath, or tries to anyway.

"You're almost 12. That's the magic number for fishing tournaments," Jim stands and picks up the suitcase. "We'll have lots of years to fish events together. Hopefully, when things are calm and steady here at home."

Gus nods, his eyebrows drawn into a scowl.

Jim tosses the remote control on the bed. "I'm not sure when I'll be back.

I'm taking this stuff to your mom, and I'll either come back tonight or tomorrow morning. Guess it'll depend on if your little sister's in a hurry or not."

The lump is thick. He can't say a word.

"Say a prayer for everybody, will you?" Jim ruffles Gus' black shiny hair, and reaches down for a hug, and whispers 'sorry' one last time, his lips so close to Gus' ear. Then, the familiar sound of footsteps on the stairs. The front door shuts, and Gus hears and feels the garage door, just underneath the bedroom.

Gus flops down on the bed, his head by the remote control. The garage door closes. Soon it is just boy and dog and a little rock and roll music on in the background.

Gus pats the bed and the old Lab loosens up his arthritic limbs and jumps up with glee. Getting invited on Mom and Dad's big bed is a huge treat. Gus sighs at Quick's enthusiasm. If only he were so easily made happy. He picks up the remote control and pushes the volume-up button. Louder. Louder still. Super loud. Quick tilts his head to the side and looks at Gus.

"What's wrong?" Gus replies to the dog's unspoken question. "I'll tell you what's wrong." His voice is loud, as he rolls over on the big bed, shouting over the still louder music—some days-gone-by rock song that Gus remembers from a *Sponge Bob, Square Pants* episode: *Born to be Wi-i-i-i-ld*.

"I make a plan, and what good does it do?" Gus asks the dog, who seems to be listening. "Work all summer for a stupid fishing tournament that I can't even do now." He picks at a scab on his right thumb. "I won't get any time with Dad. All my research and plans, finding way points and big fish presentations are toast." Can't win a tournament that you don't show up for.

Home alone, just he and the dog—Gus lets a throaty yell grow louder. "*Aaaarrrgh!*" Soon it hurts the back of his tonsils. He rolls over and curls up on his side, not even trying to stem the emotion. Somehow, letting it go feels good.

Eventually, when things are quiet, Quick moves over a little closer, putting his head right up next to Gus' cheek. The boy gently reaches for one of Quick's soft yellow ears, and touches it to his face.

"Thanks, Quickers."

He grabs the remote control and hits stop. The house goes quiet with no one else home and no music in the surround-sound system. He reaches over and pets Quick, rubbing his hand down the fullness of his back. Starting at the collar and then back down, again and again, scratching just the right spot. Tail wags. After a few minutes Gus picks himself up off the bed and stands up. Quick stands up too, and shakes hard. A bunch of loose dog hair flies all over the bed.

"Mom's not going to like that, Quick. Come on." Gus grabs the bedspread off the bed, and heads down the stairs. Feeling better, surprisingly. Out the kitchen sliding glass door to the deck, Gus shakes the dog hair off the comforter and drapes it on the deck railing. He hits at the silky fabric, allowing any remaining blonde dog hair to fall off.

"Hey," Katie calls. She's walking her bike on the sidewalk alongside the house.

"Hey," Gus replies, a little startled. He hopes his face isn't red.

"I tried to call, but there wasn't any answer."

"Oh...I, uh, didn't hear the phone. Had the music kinda loud." Still hunched over picking dog hair off the linens.

"Quite a bit to not hear the phone."

"Yeah."

"You okay?" Katie asks. "I had the feeling that you might need a friend."

Gus straightens up, but doesn't say anything. Where to start?

"My mom doesn't mind that I'm over," Katie continues. "Since your grandpa's here after school everyday."

"Well, he's in the hospital."

"There, you see? I knew something was wrong. What happened?"

"We were at the State Fair yesterday, and he collapsed with a stroke. They rushed him to the hospital and started some medications."

"I'm sorry."

"And then they did surgery last night. Put a couple of stents in."

"Oh." Katie takes in a deep breath. "Is he better?"

"I guess. I don't really know."

"So your folks are here? Or at the hospital with him?"

"That's the other things. They put my mom in the hospital. Too early for the baby to come, so she's resting with doctors' supervision."

"Wow, Gus," Katie answers. "Lots going on."

"Yeah."

"You doing okay? I mean…really okay?" Katie asks nicely.

Torn between honesty and spilling his guts, or act like everything's okay, Gus asks himself a question. What would he want from a friend? If he really cared and was asking sincerely?

"I'm not really okay, but…I just blew a little steam out with the loud music and I'm feeling better."

"Good, we all need a release, Gus. Mine's music. I play songs on the piano that fit my mood."

"Yeah, I guess. My steam-release has always been fishing, or just getting outdoors by myself. A walk in the woods or a little time in my boat. Something like that."

"That's good.

Silence.

"You want a lemonade?" Gus remembers his manners.

"Sure, as long as we sit outside. I better not go inside without…you know, parents or somebody home."

"Yeah, no problem. Hold on, I'll be right back." Gus goes inside and pours two lemonades and heads back out to the deck. He hands one to Katie.

"Thank you."

"Thanks for coming over to check on me, Katie," Gus offers. "That was nice of you." He looks away, toward the lake.

"No problem. That's what friends do for each other, right?"

"Right."

Silence

"How was school today?" Katie asks.

"Awesome that Matt Driver wasn't there, I can tell you that." Gus smiles as he says it.

"I noticed that, too," Katie laughs. "I love being the oldest in the building. So cool."

"Definitely."

"We have English class together."

"Mm-hmm."

Silence.

"You want to do some fishing? Just off the dock?"

"Sure, Gus, that'd be fun. I don't have my gear along, though."

"No worries. I have lots." He pops up from the deck chair. "Wait here, I'll be right back." With a spring in his step he returns with rods and tackle boxes enough for half a dozen people. "Have you ever fished with bottom bouncers?"

Somehow the next hour slips away, and for a few moments anyway, so do all his worries.

Chapter 5

"Really?" Gus asks, smiling into the telephone. "Tomorrow's game at Target Field? You're not kidding me?"

"I'm not kidding," Lexi replies. "What good are great connections if you can't call in a favor for your boss's own kid?" Lexi is Annie's marketing assistant for the Minnesota Twins. "Except, of course, I like getting glimpses of Joe Mauer on a regular basis. That's definitely a perk."

It is Friday afternoon and Gus was feeling just a little blue, home alone, when the phone rang. This was supposed to be the day that Gus and his dad would leave for South Dakota to pre-fish at Waubay.

"I know it's your birthday tomorrow, Gus," continues Lexi. "And that your mom's stuck at the hospital and can't get out to do any shopping for you or plan a party. Your dad's on stand-by, too. I feel a little bad for you."

"I don't usually worry about celebrating my birthday much." Gus looks down, not that Lexi could see it over the phone.

"What? I love, L-O-V-E my birthday," Lexi replies. "I celebrate for a week…sometimes a month."

"Your birthday's not 9/11." He didn't even bother to mention the connection to when Grandma Riss died.

Silence.

"I'm sorry, Gus. Didn't realize. You don't have to come down to the game tomorrow if you don't want."

"No, I do want to. This sounds fun. Thank you so much for the invitation and for thinking of me." Gus always liked Lexi when they met at the office, at a game, or on occasion when work friends came out to the lake for a barbecue or Christmas party. She had an internship with the Twins during her last year in college, studying sports marketing at the U of M. She's been there for a couple of years now.

"Okay, so I'll come out to your house tomorrow morning, pick you up at ten o'clock. Game is Noon but I have a few things I need to do, so let's get back here early. 'Kay?"

"You got it. Thanks, Lexi. I just need to clear it with my folks. They won't say no I don't think."

"They had better not," Lexi laughs. "Call me back if there's a problem. But otherwise, no news is good news."

"Okay, bye."

"Bye." Gus hangs up and immediately dials his dad's cell phone and fills him in.

"Sure, Gus," Jim says. "Sounds really fun. Glad Lexi can do all the driving. Jake is coaching the little kids' wrestling match tomorrow."

"How's Pops doing? And Mom?"

"They are both doing okay," Jim replies. "Your mom might get to come home tomorrow. They're talking about it."

"They've been talking about that for days."

"Some things just don't get scheduled, Gus. We gotta 'go with the flow' as Pops would say."

"He was kinda crabby last night when you took me in to visit."

"Maybe it will help that they're moving him to the V.A. hospital. Work on some therapy and all." Jim answers from the hallway just outside Annie's room. "Anyway, I'll be home later and we'll have dinner together. Maybe grab some Culver's?"

"Sounds good."

"I think the lawn needs mowing, buddy."

"Okay, Dad. See you later."

"Thanks, Gus. Thanks for being a good sport. I know you had some disappointment over not going out to Waubay. Appreciate your good attitude on all the change of plans, and staying on top of the work at home."

"Stuff happens."

"You're getting the hang of it. Love you, son. See you later."

Gus hangs up the phone. "Quickers," he calls the dog over, and rubs his ears. "Did you hear? There's big happenings at Target Field tomorrow, and I get to be there." Quick wags his tail. "I know. Exciting. Let's get the lawn mowed. You can help me." With a scratch on his head and ears complete, boy and dog head out the door.

Gus fills the lawn mower with gas. He grabs the pooper-scooper tool and a bucket and walks the yard picking up Quick's tell-tale signs. "Man, Quick. Seriously, this is a lot of output." Gus looks up. Quick is in hunting mode, near a clump of trees that adjoins their yard and their neighbor's.

"What's up, Quick?" Gus calls, aware of the change in Quick's demeanor. The hunting dog's body is alert. Focused. Gus walks over.

"Leave it," he calls to the dog, when he sees what it is on the ground. A baby squirrel. He looks closer. An injured or abandoned baby squirrel. It isn't moving much. "Man…what do I do?" Gus looks around, and grabs Quick by the collar and walks him to the tie-out on the other side of the house. "You stay over here for a little while," he tells the Lab. "I don't need your help on this one right now." He starts the walk back to the other side of the property, when he hears his name.

"Hey, Gus." It's Katie, on her bike.

"Hi, Katie."

"How's your mom doing? Baby yet?"

"No, not yet, which is good. Dad thinks she might come home from the hospital tomorrow." Gus walks backwards, wanting to check on the baby squirrel. But he doesn't want to be rude to Katie, either.

"That's good. And Pops?"

"Um…okay. Better." Should he tell her? "Come see this." He gestures for Katie to follow him. She does.

"Oh," Katie moans, when Gus points to the little guy. The squirrel blinks, his little heart racing, the pulse visible through his reddish-golden fur. A white mark runs half-way around his left eye. "He's so cute. But he looks so fragile…and scared."

"I'm sure he is scared."

"Is he hurt?"

"Probably."

"Well, let's take him to a vet."

"He's a wild animal, Katie."

"So, he needs help."

"I don't know, nature has a way of working things out."

"Working things out? He'll be some cat or dog's supper. That's what nature will work out for him." Katie stands up with her hands on her hips.

"Well, nature can be kind of cruel that way."

"Cornelius Gustav Roberts," Katie scolds.

"Stop using that," he shouts back, hot in less than two seconds. "And I'm not being mean. It's just…how things work." Gus has a pang of regret for yelling. Darn it, she's just so comfortable using his given name. "Why can't you just leave it alone?"

"Well, I can't believe you. Sheesh." She turns on her heel and heads back to the driveway. Gus follows and rests a hand on the lawnmower.

Katie hops on her bike and pedals away hard. Gus' heart is racing. He starts the lawn mower, the smell of the gas still on his hands. He looks over his left shoulder at the little squirrel on the ground, then proceeds to his right to start mowing on the other side of the house. A little time and space. Maybe it will be good for him and Katie just as much for this baby squirrel.

Chapter 6

"Hey there," Gus coos to the little squirrel, still in his same spot. "Your mama hasn't found you yet?" Having just finished mowing the rest of the lawn, he left the patch closest to the trees for last. His hands are still tingling from pushing the mower around for the last hour-and-a-half, even though it's off. Gus stoops down. What to do with this little guy?

"Is he okay?" Katie rides up on her bike, and hops off quickly, letting it drop to the ground with a thud.

"Yeah, he's still here anyway."

"I've been doing some research on the Internet," Katie adds, out of breath. "We need to give him some warmth. Can we use a water bottle from your recycling and fill it with warm water?"

"Sure," Gus answers, skeptical. They're talking like everything is okay.

No one moves.

Katie gives Gus a look.

"Me?" Gus asks.

"I'll keep an eye on him while you do that. Make sure no predators cause him any harm."

Gus starts to walk toward the open garage, confused.

"Not too hot, though, Gus, just tepid."

v"That's a good word, Katie," he calls out enroute to the garage.

In a moment, he returns. "Here you go. Your not-too-hot water, as requested."

"I like that word, tepid. I just learned it from my online research."

"What else did your research say?" Gus asks.

"Well, that I owe you an apology."

"Your research said that?" Gus asks.

"No, not exactly. But it said to be careful handling wild animals, and not to try to 'save them' without professional help from an animal-care center." Katie adds the quotes in the air with her hands.

Gus thought there would be a different apology. Maybe he owes one, too. Just as he's thinking on that, Katie speaks up, but this time, with a little softer tone.

"And I'm sorry I used your first name. I know you don't like it."

There. It's out there.

"We talked about it, Katie. We had a deal."

"Yeah, I just don't think it is such a big deal. Lots of people have uncommon names. It...it...just bothers you more than it should."

Even with the apology Gus is still a little needled. *Should*? Has she ever been called Corn Dog or Corny or Nelly? Katie is a perfectly ordinary name. She has no idea. Gus takes a deep breath. She did apologize.

"I'm sorry I yelled back," Gus offers. It feels right to apologize for that, too. "Okay, so we leave him alone, right?" Gus steers the conversation back to a comfort zone.

"Not exactly," Katie continues. "We add warmth; young squirrels really need that. Do you have a small cardboard box and some paper towels?" She smiles at him and Gus' stomach does a flip noticing how cute her freckles are.

"Sure," he stammers. "I'll be right back." Surprised, and glad for a little distance, he heads inside and finds a box that usually holds reams of paper in his dad's office. There's only one ream left so he takes it out and grabs a roll of paper towels from under the kitchen sink.

"Perfect," Katie compliments as he hands her his stuff out in the yard. "I brought a plastic bag and some gloves." She whips them out of her jeans pocket. "We set the plastic bag under the box to prevent moisture from entering the box. We shred the paper towel for bedding." Katie starts shredding. "Come on, you too."

Gus starts shredding the paper. "A towel would be easier and cushier. Want me to go get a rag?"

"No towels. Their toenails can get stuck in the loops of the fabric. Paper is better." She nods her head and keeps ripping up the paper towels. "I read that, too."

Gus follows suit. "You got pretty smart on this in the time it took me to mow the lawn."

"It was easy. I googled 'taking care of a baby squirrel' and saw tons of sites and articles on what to do. I read a bunch."

Gus smiles. It is exactly the kind of thing he would do. Seems they have a lot in common, even if she can be completely infuriating.

"Okay, that's enough," Katie adds, as she puts on her garden gloves. "Now we place the water bottles under the bedding, and lift him into the box." She checks that the tops are screwed on tight, and places them under the paper scraps. Then pauses.

"Well, go ahead," Gus prompts.

"I'm kind of scared."

"What?" Gus chuckles lightly. "Of that?" He points to a shivering little squirrel with big, sad brown eyes, even if one is framed with a half-swoop of white fur.

"He might be sick or diseased. My research said that, too."

"Yup. That's why you observe first. And use the gloves." Gus gestures to her light blue-clad hands.

"Oh, you're right. Here goes." Katie lifts the tiny little squirrel up into the box. "Ohhhhh…Gus."

"What?"

"He's so cute and so tiny. And his heart is racing a million miles an hour."

"I'm sure he is scared."

"Yeah. Where's his mama?"

"I don't know. Sometimes squirrels get hit on the road."

"Don't say it, Gus!" Katie strokes the little squirrel's head lightly.

"I don't know. A mother wouldn't abandon her baby without a good reason." Gus looks at Katie cooing at the frightened little squirrel. "So we leave it here?"

"Yup, it said to leave it where you find it, and hopefully the warmth and protection will give enough time for the mama to return."

"Okay, that's it I guess. Wanna come back and check on it in the morning?"

"Yes, I do. I'll come first thing," Katie answers. "But could you make sure the water bottles stay warm?"

"What? Babysit the squirrel all night?"

Katie smiles at Gus and puts her hand on his shoulder. "Just check a few times. If the bottles cool off, fill them with warmer water. You'll change it out, right?"

When she smiles, her nose wrinkles up. Gus notices. "Okay."

"Pinky promise?" She holds up her right hand in front of him and steps closer. So close Gus can smell Downy from the freshly laundered blue gardening gloves, even if the finger tips are stained dark from working in the yard.

As he links his pinky around hers, he sees his dirty hands from mowing and feels the cotton fabric on Katie's gloved hand. "Promise," he utters as he looks in her eyes. That's a promise you have to keep. Now what did Gus just get himself into?

Chapter 7

"I'm so glad to sleep here tonight," Jim says to Gus as they pull into the driveway. Double butter burgers with cheese, the tasty late-night dinner from Culver's just settling.

"I bet. Hospitals are no place to sleep I hear."

"You got that right. Lights and beeping equipment and nurses in and out all night long. They'll call if there's any need to rush down there. I'm just thankful for a night in my own bed. I'm crashing early."

"How come you're not staying at the hospital tonight, Dad?"

"The doctors have finally slowed the labor down enough, and the monitor on the baby is telling us that she's settled down and not in a big hurry."

"That's good."

"That's really good news. It's why they'll send your mom home tomorrow, hopefully. They think with rest we'll be okay and maybe get another week or two in…which is good for the baby's lungs and…well, a whole lot of things."

"I read that 36 weeks is key, out of 40. So now that we're almost 36 weeks, are they less worried?"

"Yup. Less worried, but 37 is better than 36, and 38 better than 37. Time is our friend right now."

"I don't know if Mom thinks so."

Jim smiles. "Well, yes. But she wants your little sister to have the best chance. So she'll start her maternity leave now from work. And just wait patiently at home with bed rest."

"Have you guys picked out a name yet? I only hear you say 'little sister,' not a name."

Jim sighs. "Nope. We're having a little trouble figuring it out."

"How come it's hard to pick?"

"Because we goofed up so badly on your name, that's why." Jim ruffles Gus' black shiny hair as they leave the garage. "We thought a family name celebrating our Dutch ancestors, rather famous explorers, even if they were kind of ruffians, would be kind of fun."

Gus looks away, quietly.

"But you hate it, Mr. Cornelius Gustav Roberts."

"Dad…"

"I know, Gus. Just Gus." Jim exhales as he says it.

It's quiet for a moment.

"You know Cornelius was your great-grandfather's name. Your mom's grandpa. Folks called him Nelly." Gus' stomach does a little flip. This is tender territory for a boy that likes to keep this little secret wrapped up tight. "Maybe you should come up with a name for the new baby?" Jim asks.

"Me?"

"You and Jake. Both of you come up with something. Give us some choices that you like."

"I'm okay with that."

"Good," Jim answers. "Do you have one in mind?"

"Nope, but I'll work on it."

"You do that." Jim's hand is on the door into the house.

"I've gotta check on that squirrel," Gus tells his dad, and turns to go the other direction in the yard.

"Listen, about that. I know we left a message for the local wildlife rehabilitation group. Someone will call back soon. We'll let them handle it. Okay?"

"Sure, Dad. I'm just doing some basics until we talk to them."

"Okay, well…I'm beat. I'll see you in the morning."

"Good night, Dad." Gus walks to the side yard. He peers in the cardboard box. The little guy looks okay, still small and scared, but alive. Gus feels the water bottles and decides to heat them up a little more. He makes two trips into the house so there's always one water bottle in the box. He refreshes the small dish of water, an old peanut butter jar lid. "I'm sorry your mama is still missing little guy," Gus whispers to the squirrel. "Mine is too. But at least I know where mine is." He strokes it gently. "I'll check back a couple of times." He heads back into the house, but before he climbs into bed he brushes his teeth and sets his alarm.

Beep. Beep. Beep. Louder with each tone. It only takes a couple iterations and Gus is quickly out of bed. Getting up early has always been easy for Gus. Usually because his favorite things comes after—fishing and hunting. He loves to sleep with the windows open and feel the night air. He pops up and stows a mini-flashlight in his pocket, and sighs that this early morning jaunt won't result in any nice bass or walleyes.

Down the stairs to the kitchen, where he pulls two water bottles from the recycling container near the sink. Fills them up with warm, but not-too-hot water. Tepid. He smiles and thinks of Katie, glad they smoothed things. Then heads out the side kitchen door and walks from the deck back to Squirrel Central. It's a nice night, calm. A little warm for September. Plenty of stars in the sky as he looks up. Should be a good day for baseball tomorrow, that's one good thing. Too bad he's not in South Dakota right now—preparing for a tournament. He puts the new, warmer bottles in the box and removes the cooler ones. Refraining from petting the little squirrel, Gus checks that he's alive just by sight with the light. He is. On his way back into the house he dumps the water from the bottles into his mom's flower pots on the deck, then deposits them next to the sink.

Beep. Beep. Beep. Beep. It takes a little longer at the three a.m. alarm, but he repeats his steps, filling the replacement bottles first. That makes things a little easier; one trip outside, not two. Efficient. A light breeze blows his bedroom curtains as he crawls back in the sheets.

Gus awakens again, but this time, not to the alarm. Not sure what time it is, he remains still, listening. Did he sleep through the next alarm? He looks at his clock. A little before five a.m. Nope, still too early for the birds this time of year, even they aren't up yet. 'Oh-dark-thirty' as Pops would say. Resting in bed he thinks about Webster, South Dakota. He'd be getting ready for a day of fishing with his dad right now on Lake Waubay if everything hadn't gone haywire. Prefishing for his first professional tournament. Just like you can't catch a fish without a lure in the water—you can't win a tournament without being there. Gus exhales slowly.

As he thinks on the weekend he isn't having, Gus decodes the sounds and smells of nature through the open windows. The musky scent of the lake nearby. Must be an algae bloom. Dead fish on the beach. Need to remove that before Quick finds it and rolls in it. Silly dog. Funny how even the bad smells are good smells, unless it's something your Lab has rolled in. And then he remembers. *Happy birthday to me. I'm 12 today.*

In the early hours of the morning a sound filters through the window. The *whoooo-whoooo-whoooo, who-who-who-who, whoooo-whoooo-whoooo* of a Great Horned Owl causes Gus to smile. Gus loves hearing an owl, it's not an everyday occurrence, but it happens once in awhile. A visit from a Great Horned Owl is a special sound. Gus mentally checks his animal name game knowledge. A baby owl is a fledgling. Suddenly, *crap!*

He tears out of bed and bolts down the stairs, tripping over Quick. He doesn't stop at the sink, and nearly pulls the sliding glass door off its track as he dashes as fast as he can to the box. Is he too late? What will Katie say if her little buddy is gone? *Crud.*

Chapter 8

The hair on the back of Gus' neck stands up as he looks down at the cardboard box. Moonlight is interrupted as a huge black shadow crosses overhead. A b-i-g shadow. Silently, the Great Horned Owl flying overhead creates only a sensation, not a sighting. They are stealthy like Ninjas.

"Oh man, you're okay," Gus mutters to the little squirrel, with a big exhale. "Come on. You're going in the garage." Gus picks up the box and enters the house through the same door that he came out, by the deck. He's about to head through the kitchen to the mud room and then to the garage, when his dad flips on a light. He's in his boxers with a baseball bat in his right hand.

"What's going on? What's the matter?" Jim looks left and right.

"Sorry, Dad. Didn't mean to wake you."

"It sounded like a herd of elephants on the stairs."

"It was me…I was in a panic."

"What's wrong?" He drops the bat down to his side.

"I heard a Great Horned Owl, and realized our little squirrel-friend would be his breakfast if I didn't protect him a little better." Gus hefts the box a little higher. "So, he's going to the garage until morning."

"I thought you weren't supposed to move them from where you found them."

"Dad, he'd be easy pickings for an owl."

"Yeah, that's nature," Jim grumbles. "I suppose. Go ahead, put him in the garage."

Gus does, and returns.

"Back to bed?" Jim asks.

"Yeah, I'll put him back outside in the morning. Katie's coming over to check on him. I'm just going to refill his water bottles first." Gus walks toward the sink, bottle in hand.

"Are you doing the right thing here? It's more than I would have guessed." Jim runs his hands through his hair, and harrumphs while he retreats back up the stairs. "Go back to bed."

Gus shrugs his shoulders in the dark kitchen and mumbles. *Happy birthday to me. Not.*

"Lexi, this is Katie. Katie, Lexi." Gus, clad in his Twins shirt and hat, introduces the gals in the driveway a few hours later.

"Nice to meet you," Lexi replies as she offers her hand for a handshake.

Katie responds formally. "Nice to meet you, too. So…you work with Gus' mom?"

"Mmm-hmm. We've worked together for about five years now. Kinda grown to like this family—especially Gus. Got great seats at the game for his birthday."

"It's your birthday today?" Katie looks over at Gus, her mouth agape.

"Uh, yeah," he replies as he turns his back. "Shall we go?" he asks Lexi.

"Sure, Gus. Bye, Katie. It was nice to meet you." Lexi hops in her car.

"I'll be right back," Gus slinks away, ignoring the dirty look from Katie. "I need to grab my sign." In a moment, Gus returns from the garage with his Cecil Owen sign. It has a big photo on it.

Katie hops on her bike and begins to pedal away. "Happy birthday, Gus," she hollers brusquely.

"Funny, when she says it, she doesn't sound very happy," Lexi chuckles, as Gus hops in and closes the car door.

"Don't worry about it. She's just not happy 'cuz she didn't know it was my birthday."

"You keepin' it on the down low?" Lexi backs out of the driveway.

Gus doesn't say anything. The car is quiet while Lexi recalls the previous night's phone conversation. Gus' birthday is on the 11th of September.

She never really thought about what it would be like to have a birthday on that day. She's known friends who have birthdays that sometimes fall on Thanksgiving or same day as Valentines Day. But 9/11? Every flag is at half-mast. It is such a somber and patriotic day, so filled with lives lost. "I think I understand better now." She smiles at him. "It is a beautiful day for baseball, though."

"Yes it is," Gus replies, glad for the change in subject.

"Um…Gus…" Lexi hesitates. "There will be some 9/11 stuff at the game today."

"Oh, that's okay, Lexi. I want to focus on that today."

"You got it."

Silence.

"You're kind of a complicated kid, Gus."

What she says hangs in the air.

"My promise is to never forget," Gus finally replies, quietly.

"You've thought about this a lot, haven't you, Gus."

"I guess. It's been a part of my life since I was just a baby."

"Too little to really even remember that day."

"True that. But we've talked about it at home."

"So you won't mind a tribute at Target Field?"

"No, I won't mind at all. I would love that," Gus replies. "I just don't want today to be about my birthday. Like up on the board or anything."

Silence.

"You weren't going to do that, were you?" Gus asks.

No reply.

"L-e-x-i?"

"I'll take it down. I was adding two and two and getting six. Sorry." Lexi shrugs her shoulders.

"Pinky promise?"

She holds up her right hand in a stopping gesture, flips open her phone and calls her office. "Take out the birthday greeting for Gus on the big board, please." Lexi listens for a moment. "Uh-huh. I'm sure." She listens some more. "You sure it's out? Deleted? 100%? Okay, thanks." She closes her phone and tosses it back on top of her purse.

"Promise." She downshifts around a corner and moves her right hand from the shifter to Gus' offered digit. The two break out in giggles as they shake on it.

But there are two more 9/11 surprises waiting for Gus at Target Field. He just doesn't know anything about them yet. And for one of them, neither does Lexi.

Chapter 9

"Wow, these are great seats, Lexi," Gus exclaims, settling in near the Twins' dugout, first row behind first base.

"I know, I love the view." Lexi sighs as she watches some of the Twins toss balls to each other as they warm up. Joe Mauer and Justin Morneau to name a few.

"This stadium is so awesome. It has to be the nicest in the country."

"Well, it is one of the newest in the country," Lexi replies, sitting up tall. "We can be very proud of our baseball stadium in Minnesota. It's just as good, if not better, than any other."

"I totally agree. I like it when the Twin players, St. Paul and Minneapolis, shake hands when there's a home run."

"I like that, too. And I love how beautiful the skyline of Minneapolis is, tucked all around the stadium. And how the plaza connects the stadium to the city."

Gus puts his sign on the floor under his seat. "And they have the best kettle corn."

"Oh, I should buy you something to eat, shouldn't I?" Lexi looks around for stadium vendors, but it's a little early.

"That's okay, I brought some money."

"Are you sure? I need to cover off on a few things before the game starts. I'll be back, but it might not be until a couple of innings in. Be sure you're watching for the National Anthem okay?"

"Of course."

"I mean it. Don't miss it." Lexi stands.

Gus looks at Lexi. "I won't miss it."

"You okay on your own? Just stay put and don't get lost."

"Lexi, where else would I want to be than right here?"

"Okay, back when I can." Lexi takes the steps two at a time up to the main concourse.

Gus enjoys watching the pre-game relaxed atmosphere. These up-front seats give a great view of the players. People arrive and fill in all around him. Too bad Pops isn't here. He would love these seats.

Thinking of Pops and his move to the V.A. hospital reminds Gus of the sign that he brought. If he's lucky enough, Pops will be watching the game on television and see him with it. That's why he brought it, after all. And then he sees Cecil Owen and some of the media crew down on the field. They're walking toward the Twins' dugout, casually shaking hands and saying hello to the players and the coaching staff. *Should I?* Gus wonders. He reaches down and picks up the sign, stands tall with it over his head. The somewhat-famous catcher from back in the day, now TV announcer, sees it and chuckles. He walks over.

With a red marker in his hand, he leans the short distance into the first row of seats to mark up Gus' poster. Other people all around are calling out, saying hello.

"Hey, I know that old guy," Cecil Owen replies as he points to the photo on Gus' sign. "That's Hessel Riss—Pops."

Gus nearly drops it. "Mr. Owen, you know Pops?"

"Sure do. I've been pheasant hunting in South Dakota with Pops, and up to Leech Lake in his plane. Used to go fishing with him and his wife, Weezer years back when our daughters were the same age. Everybody knew those two—Hessel and Louise. Friends called them Pops and Weezer. We both adopted daughters from Korea a long time ago. Our girls are friends and grew up together."

"Annie's my mom."

"Wow. I should have guessed. You look just like her. That makes you Jake or Gus," Mr. Owen replies.

"Gus." Hard to believe he knew Gus' name.

"Nice to meet you, Gus." He finishes circling Pops' picture on the sign with the requisite "Cecil Owen" greeting above it. Gus had used a large marker next to Pops' picture and written "Get better, come home soon" below it.

"Pops is in the hospital?" Cecil Owen asks.

"Stroke."

"That's too bad. Will he still be able to fly his plane?"

"His plane's been grounded, left up at Leech Lake since May—after he lost his medical rating. I don't know what he'll do with it. Sell it maybe."

"But he'll be okay?" the retired pro asks.

"He's recuperating, one side is affected more than the other. They put in two stents a few days ago. He's at the Veterans hospital."

"Pops was a brave naval aviator back in the day. How's your mom? She here with you today?"

"She's in the hospital, too. Baby might be coming early."

"Wow. Lots going on."

"Yeah."

"Hey Justin, toss me one," the TV-personality catcher calls to the first baseman nearby. Justin Morneau tosses Mr. Owen a ball. He jots a note with the red marker. "Give this to Pops for me."

"Will do. Thank you Mr. Owen."

"And Gus? Give your mom and dad my best, too."

"Will do, sir. And thank you, Mr. Owen."

"Call me Cecil. We're not that formal around here. In fact, tell your mom if she has the baby today she needs to name him Cecil."

"It's a girl, sir."

Cecil laughs. "Okay. Then Cece, short for…I don't know…Cecelia." He chuckles.

As Cecil Owen walks away, everyone around Gus asks to see the baseball and what it says. It's a little odd for a signature. It doesn't say anything about baseball, just—'Fishin'… soon. Cecil'. Some of the folks around him act disappointed. Not Gus. His opinion of Cecil Owen, which was high before, just shot through the roof.

"My grandfather goes hunting and fishing with Cecil Owen," he says to the guy to his right, who nods. Even the grandma that he never had a chance to know, went fishing with big league baseball players. Grandma Louise…and they called her Weezer. How about that.

Chapter 10

"Ladies and gentlemen," the stadium speakers erupt, with instructions from the Master of Ceremonies. "Near the conclusion of the National Anthem, an American Bald Eagle named Challenger, will soar down onto the field."

Gus looks down near home plate and sees Lexi. They make eye contact and she smiles.

"Challenger is a non-releasable Bald Eagle cared for by the non-profit American Eagle Foundation, headquartered at Dollywood, in Pigeon Forge, Tennessee," the emcee continues. "He is named in honor of the Space Shuttle crew."

Gus is on his feet, looking upward, as are most in the stadium.

"Challenger was blown from a wild nest as a baby during a storm, and was hand-raised by the people who rescued him," the emcee continues. "Unfortunately, he experienced too much human contact at a very young age and became human socialized. As a result, Challenger thinks he's a person and cannot survive on his own in the wild. He is cared for by the American Eagle Foundation under federal and state permits for education purposes."

"Wow," the guy on Gus' right replies.

"Acting as an ambassador for his species, Challenger has raised a great level of national public awareness about the need to restore and protect America's eagles, natural resources and environment. The Bald Eagle is still a protected species throughout the United States, and much of its nesting and feeding habitat is being encroached upon by humans," the emcee reads while the cameras pan to the singer, standing in front of the microphone. "Let's keep America's eagles flying strong and free."

The crowd roars.

"Please rise and remove your caps, as we pledge to never forget, on this anniversary of 9/11. Kelly Johnson will sing the Star Spangled Banner—the National Anthem of the United States of America."

Gus is already on his feet, cap in one hand at his left side, right hand over his heart. Everyone else is at their feet, too. Even folks on the stairs stop and stand still out of respect.

"Oh, say, can you see," Kelly begins the song. She has a beautiful crystal-clear voice, and eyes that sparkle as she sings. "By the dawn's early light…"

Gus listens to Kelly, standing at attention. He lets his eyes wander to where a huge flag is unfurled in the center of the stadium, in the outfield. More than forty soldiers in dress uniform hold the edges of the material and step quickly to showcase the red, white and blue. A color guard is also nearby, presenting arms.

"What so proudly we hail'd, at the twilight's last gleaming?" she continues, as her face is plastered all over the Jumbotron screens.

Gus is caught up in the moment. He feels it each and every time the National Anthem is sung. There's a special passion today, that makes the hairs on his arm stand up, as he remembers the threat that struck America on 9/11…when Gus was just a baby.

"Whose broad stripes and bright stars, thro' the perilous fight. O'er the ramparts we watch'd, were so gallantly streaming? And the rockets' red glare…"

Fireworks leap out of the corners of the stadium, bright lights and big sounds.

"The bombs bursting in air…gave proof thro' the night, that our flag was still there."

A lump rises up in Gus' throat, but he pushes it down.

"Oh say does that star spangled banner yet wave. O'er the land of the free…" Kelly does a beautiful soprano hold on this note and now the hair stands up on the back of Gus' neck.

"And the home…"

Several seconds before the song finishes, the eagle swoops high above the stadium, circling. Then he races down at a tremendous speed, flying over the wind-tossed American flag. He soars around the stadium, the outstretched wingspan h-u-g-e.

"...of the," Kelly continues singing.

Gus' eyes open wide, as does his mouth. He knew the flight of the eagle was coming, but he didn't know how spectacular it would be. He hears "Oh how beautiful," and "Look," from people all around him.

There's no way he can take his eyes off of this bird of prey. He is exquisite in every way, radiating a magnetic power that draws Gus in. Watching.

Gus didn't realize he was holding his breath, and exhales before taking in a big lungful of air. The eagle flies near him, so near Gus can see the white head and tail feathers that contrast with the near-black body. There's the strong, yellow, sharp-hooked bill; and the talons have long, razor-sharp claws.

He can't hold it down. The lump that was there before rises to the top, and he doesn't even try to stop it. Pride, deep-rooted pride of being an American, swells. He's caught up with emotion as the soldiers hold the flag and present arms. Thinking about all the families who lost loved ones on 9/11 so many years ago, and all the first responders who lost their lives trying to help, the corners of Gus' eyes well up.

Not far from where Gus is sitting, the eagle swoops low to the grassy field, then pulls his wings back in a motion that must be like applying brakes for a bird of prey.

"Braaaaaaaave," the singer concludes with a long soprano hold.

Challenger lands with his talons on a waiting man's gloved, outstretched arm—timed with the last words of the anthem. He sits tall, head erect. Smart eyes—eagle eyes—look all around, taking in his surroundings. The stadium erupts in cheers. Gus looks over at the singer, and she, too, is overcome.

"Oh my goodness," the man next to Gus bursts forth, whacking Gus on the shoulder. "Have you ever seen anything more beautiful in all your life?" The man's voice is shaking. He wipes his eyes.

Gus nods, and discreetly wipes his cheek with right elbow as he puts his cap back on. Takes a big breath and exhales slowly, pulling himself back together.

The announcer is back on the loud speakers. "Ladies and gentlemen, let's give Challenger and his handler, Al Cecere, a Target Field welcome."

The stadium explodes with applause, and Gus is part of it, too. The man the announcer just introduced, turns a 360, allowing everyone a chance to see Challenger. Camera flashes explode like millions of fireflies on a summer night.

Gus spots Lexi next to Al Cecere and Challenger. She escorts them both to a side door near the dugouts, but before they disappear, Mr. Cecere waves good-bye to the stadium crowd. As he does, Lexi makes eye contact with Gus again. She smiles big, and her eyes twinkle. Then, with a wink, she disappears into the bowels of Target Field.

Gus is alone in his moment amongst tens of thousands. But it definitely is a moment. Time to think about the beauty of the bird—the American Bald Eagle—and the beauty of the National Anthem. And the freedoms that both represent.

Challenger. What an amazing eagle with an unusual name. Gus is reminded of a name idea for the baby sister that will soon be here. He's had a couple of ideas recently. What were they again? Oh yeah. He tries it on in his head and rolls it around his tongue.

"So cool to honor the crew from the Space Shuttle," Lexi replies a little later. Gus was quick with a question as soon as she sat down at the beginning of the third inning.

"That all happened before I was born," Gus says. "Was it a really sad day, like 9/11?"

"Yes, it really was," Lexi replies. "I was just a little girl when it happened, but I remember being at school and all the teachers crying. Seven people were killed—the entire crew."

"I need to read up on it," Gus replies. "I'm not familiar with all the facts around the Challenger explosion."

"Well, I'm glad you liked seeing Challenger the eagle."

"I liked it a lot, Lexi. Thank you for these tickets. This is a great day."

"Gus Roberts," Lexi looks over at him. "Really?"

"Yes, really. I'm enjoying being at the game and no one knows about you-know-what, except you."

"Except me, but I'm not mentioning it."

"Right. And it's all about baseball and our country...and what happened on 9/11."

"I was worried you wouldn't like all the attention to it."

The two enjoy their kettle corn and sodas while watching the game.

"Did they try to release Challenger back to the wild?" Gus asks.

"Yup, two times. And he only looked to humans to feed him, not to nature. It was pretty scary to have him approach random humans looking for food. Some were very scared to have this eagle fly up close to them. One almost killed him in the process. Challenger got really weak and emaciated."

"Wow, I suppose."

"Sometimes people can be well-intentioned but still make a mistake."

Gus thinks about the squirrel with the white ring around one eye in his yard. "But in a way, I'm kind of glad that Challenger has been trained to do special events like this one," Gus continues. "If he were a free eagle, we'd never see him up close in a stadium during the National Anthem. And with no intervention at all, he probably would have died."

"That's true. It was a very special event, don't you think?"

"Definitely. Good thinking to organize it, Lexi."

Lexi laughs. "Oh, your mom organized this one."

"Really?" Gus smiles. "I didn't know."

"I'm just glad I could help out. And I'm glad that you were able to be here."

"It was awesome."

"I felt it in the whole stadium, Gus. Totally amazing."

Gus shows Lexi the signed ball from Cecil Owen.

"Cool," she replies.

"I guess I'm finding surprises out about my mom and the Riss side of the family today," Gus answers. "I wonder how they are doing?"

Indeed, big changes have happened today back at the hospital, but when will Gus find out what's going on?

Chapter 11

"Mom?" Gus calls as he runs into the house.

"Upstairs," Annie calls out.

"You're home!" Gus exclaims, as he enters the master bedroom and runs to the side of the bed. Annie opens her arms wide and he launches in for a bear hug.

"Whoa, you're getting strong, Gus," Annie replies. "Easy."

"Just excited to have you home," Gus says as he lets go.

"How was the game? And happy birthday."

"Thanks. The game was great, even if we lost. Lexi got us super-amazing seats. Right by first base, first row."

"Wow."

"And I saw Challenger, the Bald Eagle. Mom, that was so cool."

"Glad you liked it. I wish I could have been there to see him at Target Field. I saw him in Kansas City last year."

"And I met Cecil Owen, and he knows you and Pops. He autographed a baseball and gave it to me to give to Pops."

"I heard."

"How'd you hear."

"Lexi called me to tell me she was taking you to the V.A. hospital to visit Pops, and deliver the autographed ball. I told her we were on our way home from the hospital, too."

"How's the baby?"

"She's settled down and I just need to take it easy. How was Pops tonight?"

"He's having trouble with his left side. But his right side is working pretty good. His face looks a little droopy, though. And his left eye seems...I don't know...sad."

"That's what can happen with a stroke."

"His speech is coming along, just a little slow. And when he walks his left leg drags a little bit."

"It'll take a little time and therapy."

"Where's Dad? And Jake?" Gus asks.

"Jake is at a movie with Amanda tonight."

"Oh yeah?"

Annie smiles and nods. "And Dad went to the store to stock up on some food. Some easy things that he can make and things I can heat up for leftovers since I'll be home more."

"So...you're kinda stuck here? In bed now?"

"Kinda."

"Bummer." Gus looks through the window blinds.

"Yeah, well...it'll just be a few weeks. If I can get two or three more weeks in, everything will be better."

The two hear the rumble of the garage door under the bedroom floor. "Dad's home."

"Go help him with the groceries, Gus. You know the rule, right?"

"Yeah. If you want to eat any of it, you'd better put it away."

Annie chuckles. "Your choice—schlep it or pay for it. Thanks, buddy. I'm so glad to have your help around here."

"What happened to the squirrel, Dad? I see he's gone," Gus asks his father as the grocery bags are set on the kitchen floor.

"I don't know. Katie left a note saying she was taking it in."

"Really?"

"I guess so," Jim replies. "You worried about a squirrel, Gus?"

"No. Well...a little. He was kinda cute, Dad. And he looked so helpless." Jim chuckles softly and shakes his head. "Gus..."

"It was kinda Katie's project, Dad."

"Sorry I was a little crabby about it this morning," Jim replies. "You know, the owl thing at oh-dark-thirty."

Silence. Gus loads the canned goods into the pantry pull-out shelves.

"And happy birthday, Gus. You're 12."

"I am glad to be 12, Dad. It makes a lot of difference." Gus puts the milk in the door of the refrigerator, and tries not to think about the fact that he and his dad should be in South Dakota, pre-fishing for a team-format tournament on a sweet little walleye lake—Waubay. All summer long he worked to save up money for this special event. Between the pre-fish and the tournament he'd get two weekends on Waubay. Now he's not getting anything. He's been counting down the days to turning 12 so he could fish a professional-level tournament. And with all that's going on around here and his extra chores, he's not even getting out on the water on Lake Minnetonka, his own back yard. He hasn't been fishing with his friends Asher and Doogie even once this September. His hands, normally scratched and rough from handling fish, are now clean of scabs. They don't look like fisherman fingers at all—and Gus doesn't like that.

"Since you have your boat license, you can drive the big boat now."

Gus smiles just a little bit thinking about that news. There's one plus about being 12. "Oh yeah. Will you let me take the Ranger Boat out by myself? Now that I can, legally and all?"

"Sometimes. You'll have to ask each time. Our new boat is arriving any day. Bruce Driver is buying this boat from us."

"Matt Driver's dad?"

"Yup. And don't get mad at me if you can't reach me in two seconds for an answer and you have to use the *Plywood Princess* instead." The *Plywood Princess* is Gus' small boat with a 15-horse Johnson.

"It'll be hard to go back to my boat after driving the Ranger 620 or the newer one."

"True. But it isn't your boat. It's my boat—and you'll need to ask permission to use it."

Gus folds the last of the reusable grocery bags, varying colors of green and red, processing the reality that Matt Driver (of all people!) will have *their* Ranger 620 to use. The Labrador, Quick, is nearby and drops a ball at his feet, anxious for someone to play with him. Gus picks up the ball and tosses into the living room. Quick runs for it.

Jim walks over to the stairs. "Come on Mr. Twelve-year-old. Let's go up and see if your mom needs anything." The Lab brings up the rear—ball in mouth.

"I have a birthday present for you, Gus." Annie pats the bed, after finishing the dinner the guys brought up for her. Gus sits down on the edge. "It might be a little unconventional, but I think you'll like it." Annie nods at Jim, and he slips out of the room. Gus can hear footfalls on the stairs.

"Mom, we usually do presents later—on the 12th or 13th or something."

"I know." Annie is very aware of her son's sensitivity to having his birthday on 9/11. "You've had a fun day today, right?"

"Yes. Very fun."

"So, I think this will be a nice way to end your evening."

Silence.

"Do you trust me Gus Roberts?"

"Yes, Mom." Gus looks over his shoulder.

Jim re-enters the room quietly, arms tucked behind his back. Gus' radar is on high alert.

"What's going on?" Gus asks.

"Well…I haven't been able to do any shopping lately."

"I know. That's not a big deal for me. You know that."

"So I decided on a different kind of gift. Something that belongs to me. It was once a gift your father gave to me, and now I'm giving it to you."

Gus' eyes sparkle. The clue is making his heart race. Is this what he thinks it is? Oh my goodness, if it is? Better not get his hopes up.

"You were just a baby, so you probably don't remember the day, but when your dad turned thirty I gave him a very special present on his birthday."

"I remember the story, Mom. You gave him the Silver Pigeon," Gus replies. "It's one of his favorite shotguns."

"It is," Annie smiles over at Jim. "He thought it was the best present a person could ever get. And he was so happy, that when I turned thirty a few years later, he gave me one just like it." She chuckles. "Somehow I wasn't quite as thrilled as he was…"

"Matching Berettas. Only yours is a 20-gauge." Gus may have been little, but it was a big deal to get a present like that. He remembers, and tries to grab hold of his emotions. *Settle down, don't get ahead of yourself.* He tries to manage expectations.

"Right."

Silence. Gus' palms are sweaty, he wipes them on his khaki shorts. Is she doing what he thinks she's doing? He smiles. "Mom?"

"So…" Annie seems to be enjoying drawing the suspense along. She looks over at Jim and nods. "I'm giving you my shotgun. Happy birthday, son," Annie says.

Gus jumps up off the bed. He leaps in the air, his feet busy with a happy dance, like some NFL-player would do in an end zone after scoring a touchdown. He fist pumps the air. "YES!!!!"

Jim walks over from the doorway, the beautiful shotgun revealed as he pulls off a cloth sock-sleeve. Gus stops goofing and when he does, Jim hands it over to him. Gus handles it carefully, the muzzle always away and not pointing at anyone. He stands tall, his big smile revealing straight, white teeth. His brown eyes sparkle with glee, and his cinnamon-brown skin, a little lighter in tone than his mother's darker Asian skin, flushes red with all the activity. The first thing he does is push the lever to the right, opening the breech. He confirms the gun is empty. Yup, empty. Even though Gus trusts his dad not to carry a loaded firearm around and hand it to someone, he's also had it drilled into his head that every time, EVERY TIME someone hands you a gun that's the first thing you check. Even if the one handing you the gun is the dad who drilled the very lesson into your head.

Jim nods with approval. Gus has passed the test—again. Just once, two years ago, when Jim handed Gus a firearm in a similar fashion, Gus failed to check it. He was grounded for an entire month. No boat privileges—not even the *Plywood Princess*. And he had to stack firewood from a tree that fell in a storm. That was hard work in the heat of the summer. It took a whole month to work out his consequence.

"You're 12 now, Gus. And your mother thinks you can handle this responsibility. Can you?"

"Oh yes, Dad. You know I can."

"You'll be careful?" Annie asks. "Follow all the rules you learned in Firearms Safety Training?"

"That…and everything Dad's taught me too. You've got it."

"Keep it unloaded unless you're afield." Jim adds.

"Yup."

"Keep it locked up in the gun safe at home, unless you're cleaning it. And I'm the keeper of the safe keys," Jim adds.

"Yup. Yup." Gus runs his fingers along the dark walnut stock, taking in the warm brownish-red tones of the rich wood grain. He touches the swirly etchings of pheasants in the scroll artwork, envisioning his first opportunity to carry this gun while pheasant hunting. And duck hunting. "This is so beautiful. Thank you, Mom." Gus moves the shotgun to his left hand and reaches across his mother with his right. He hugs her tight, the best that he can with one arm. While he's in close for the hug, he whispers in her ear: "Thank you, Mom. I love it."

Annie smiles, and little tears well up in her eyes. "I can't believe how big you are now, Gus. Big enough for this privilege. Look how tall you are." She grabs a tissue from the night stand and dabs at her dark brown eyes.

Gus smiles.

"And it is a privilege, Gus," Jim barks, with a bit of an edge to his voice. Gus turns his head abruptly to his dad sitting on the corner of the bed—the mood of the fun moment clipped. "If you mishandle it, or if your behavior in any way, ANY WAY, tells us that you aren't mature enough for this privilege, it will be revoked."

Gus looks at his dad, squarely. "I know that."

"Okay." Jim casts a stern glance.

"Okay." Gus holds the glance with his own. Equally serious. A meeting of the minds. Two seconds pass that feel like an eternity.

"Okay, okay, already." Annie lightens the tone. "I have just one favor to ask."

"What's that?" Breaking the stare down with his father, Gus turns his gaze back to his mom.

"Let me borrow it back when your dad and I shoot some sporting clays. I love this gun for clays."

"And your mother is an eagle-eye with it," Jim offers, settling into a more relaxed mood, the tension lifted.

"I can't out-shoot your father," Annie smiles as she says it. "But as a couple, we usually come in first place in a clays competition. We're pretty hard to beat."

"We are. You're a good partner," Jim stands up and kisses her on her forehead. "Come on, Gus. Let's put that away for the night. Time for bed."

Gus stands up and smiles. "Thanks, Mom. I'll take good care of it for you. And you can borrow it anytime you want."

Annie smiles, and reaches over for the light on the nightstand next to the bed. She turns it off. "Catch the big light on your way out guys. Good night." She settles her big round body under the covers, and fluffs a pillow up under her head.

Jim flicks the light switch off and the room darkens quickly. He pulls the door closed, to minimize any noise or light entering. "Sleep tight," he speaks softly. Two men walk down the stairs together. For one, holding his new prized possession, it is the first moment that he feels like a man.

Chapter 12

"So Peanut's doing okay." Katie informs, on the bus ride home from school a few days later. Somedays Katie gives Gus the cold shoulder. Today it seems all is well.

"Peanut?"

"You know. The baby squirrel."

"You named him?" Reminds Gus of something on his to-do list, a name for his baby sister.

"Yup. Peanut."

"Sheesh, Katie. You're not supposed to get so connected to a wild animal."

"He wasn't all that wild. Pretty tame, actually."

"What do you mean—tame?"

"Well, I spent quite a bit of time with him on Saturday when you were at the baseball game. He liked being petted. And eating peanuts."

"You fed him?" Gus' eyes open wide.

"Yup. My mom said they won't pick them up, you have to drive them in. It was taking so long I figured the little guy needed some food and water. He liked the peanuts." Katie shrugs her shoulders.

"I don't think you're supposed to do that, Katie."

"I know. All the research said to leave them alone. But I just couldn't." Katie's eyes look soft and tender—like a puppy or even a baby squirrel's.

Gus looks away. Out the window is better, no puppy eyes there. She can be so frustrating, and so cute at the same time. He doesn't say anything until the bus stops at his corner. "I gotta go. See you Monday. You, too, Marsha. Bye." He gives a little wave with his right hand and a quick "bye, Linda" to the bus driver.

Quick doesn't greet him at the door when he arrives. He kicks off his shoes and sets them neatly under his cubby in the foyer. It's quiet. No smells of freshly baked anything. Sure is different without Pops around. Where is Quick anyway?

"Mom?" Gus calls out, a bit hesitantly. Doesn't want to startle her if she's sleeping. He listens from the bottom of the stairs. No answer. He moves into the kitchen and locates the English muffins, pulls one apart and drops it in the toaster. While the two halves are toasting, Gus grabs the Jif. Quick runs in to greet him.

"Hi Quickers."

Quick breathes heavily, panting.

"What's the matter? You gotta go outside?" The warm bread-halves pop up from the toaster, and Gus spreads on the peanut butter treat. "Just a minute," Gus stalls the Lab. He sits down at the island on a stool and takes a bite. Quick is prancing. Dancing even.

"What is the matter with you?" Gus asks the dog. "You looking for a treat?" He offers a bite of the warm, peanutty after-school treat, but Quick wriggles and moans, stepping backwards out of the kitchen.

What's wrong with this picture? Quick never turns down people food. "Man, you must have to pee." Gus walks the other direction to the kitchen sliding glass door and holds it open for the dog. "Okay, Quick, outside." Gus calls. But the dog doesn't follow. He's still on the other side of the kitchen, toward the hallway and stairs. Now the dog is vocalizing, a kind of doggie-warble.

"Quick, come!" Gus calls. The Lab comes as summoned and sits down in front of Gus. "Okay." Gus motions with the door wide open, but the dog doesn't head outdoors. Instead, he warbles and dances back toward the stairway.

"What?" Gus asks, as he closes the slider and follows. The following seems to make Quick happy, and the dog heads up the stairs to the first landing. More girations.

"You want me to follow you?" Gus asks, and does. Quick is very happy now, prancing a dance in the hallway, turning and vocalizing to his boy. "Okay, okay." Gus says as he follows. Quick pushes the master bedroom door wide open, and continues all the way back to the bathroom. "Mom?" Gus calls out, hesitant to follow the dog into the private space. She's not in her bed like the other days this week. Usually Gus would find her resting, doing crossword puzzles and cryptoquotes on her Kindle. Gus stands there for a few seconds, listening for any noise.

Totally quiet. Quick returns from the bathroom with more dancing and warbling antics. The dog darts back into the bathroom, with turning, twisting motions.

Hesitantly, Gus calls out "Mom?"

With no answer, he peeks around the door into the large bathroom, following the dog. "Mo…" Gus' call gets swallowed in his throat. His mother is lying on the floor of the bathroom. She's in a heap on the rug.

"Mom, are you okay?" Gus rushes to her side. No response.

He runs back to the bedroom and grabs the cordless phone on the nightstand. Until ten days ago he had never, ever dialed nine-one-one before. Suddenly, this is the second time in two weeks that's he's needed emergency services. *Lord, dear Lord…help my mom and this new baby sister be alright.* He punches the third digit.

"It's my mom," Gus tells the dispatcher. "She's passed out, and she's pregnant."

"Can you get her to the hospital?"

"No. We need an ambulance."

They cover off on some details and Gus hangs up the phone. "They're on their way," Gus murmurs to his Mom, a catch in his voice.

Every second ticks off in Gus' head as he watches his mom on the floor next to him. The rise and fall of her body show's that she's breathing. Her belly is big—full of baby sister. Her face is red and she's hot to his touch. He brushes a bit of long, shiny black hair away from her face. *God, please keep both of them safe.* He opens a drawer and wets a washcloth with cool water. He bends back down and places it on her forehead and temples.

Dad. Tell Dad. Gus remembers he's up shooting on-the-water photos for a magazine cover. Where was he going? Leech? That's more than three hours away if he was in his truck right this minute. And Jim's probably on the water getting different angles of the boat and the fisherman with a grip-n-grin big fish shot for the photo shoot.

Quick barks, breaking the stillness, and jumps up to leave the room. "They're here," Gus says as he rises.

Gus' stocking feet *kalunk-kalunk-kalunk* down the stairs, so fast it's nearly a free-fall. Quick is at the front door, barking. Gus arrives and opens the door to the paramedics. He holds Quick back with his left hand. "She's upstairs, first door on the left. In the bathroom."

Two paramedics rush upstairs, one carrying a case—kind of a big tackle box. Gus isn't sure if he should follow or not, but after a second or two of indecision commits to head upstairs. He lingers in the bedroom, not too far away from the commotion.

Soon, Annie is on a gurney and the emergency response crew is wheeling her toward the doorway.

"You riding along?" One of the paramedics asks Gus, as the legs fold up under the bed-on-wheels as they go down the stairs.

"Uh…yeah," Gus replies. He scans the room, and grabs his mother's cell phone and tosses it in his pocket. A thought jumps into his head. How do you pay for an ambulance ride? He opens her purse and grabs her photo ID, credit card and insurance card. When his eye spots the charger plugged into the wall just a few feet away, he grabs that, too. He brings up the rear as the group is now out the front door. Turns to Quick. "Be good," he tells the sad-eyed Labrador. "I'll be home when I can." He closes the door behind him.

"Ride up front," the paramedic instructs, and slams the back door in Gus' face. Gus dashes to the right side of the vehicle, and he climbs into the front passenger seat and closes the door. As the ambulance departs with a *woop-woop-woop* Gus wonders what can he do to help. *Think, Gus, think.* He's never felt more helpless before in his life.

Chapter 13

"Perfect. Hold the largemouth up just a little more. That's it."

Jim clicks the fancy digital camera multiple times. He's already taken hundreds of photos today, leaning over the edge of his Ranger Boat.

"A little more light on his face," Jim calls out to his assistant, who's standing in the front of Jim's boat. The assistant's holding a shiny-golden fabric circle, bouncing light up on the pro-angler's face.

Jim is taking the shot from about six feet away in his own boat. The beginnings of the seasonal color change are in the trees in the background, various shades of orange and yellow mixed in with all the green. This is a nice secluded spot with no houses or docks in the background. A little slice of nature away from civilization. Then a noise breaks through the quiet. It gets louder and louder.

"What the heck?" Jim asks, as he cranes his neck around.

The noise gets louder and louder! Jim looks up and can't believe what he sees. All of sudden the water around his boat casts a circular pattern of wind ripples. A helicopter is hovering just above the two boats.

"Hey!" Jim's photography assistant yells, thinking the helicopter doesn't see them directly below. The downdraft is strong and stuff starts flying around in the boat. He grabs at a towel before it lands in the lake, and struggles mightily with the round light reflector panel he's holding.

But the guys are wrong thinking this pilot doesn't see them. The helicopter is just where the pilot wants it to be. And it hovers closer and closer to the two boats. Closer still. Now hovering just above the empty bow of the pro's boat where no one is standing.

"What's going on?" the fisherman yells over the noise of the rotor blades, with the bass in his hand. He opens the livewell and tosses the bass inside, all the while keeping his head bent low.

"I don't know!" Jim has to shout to be heard over the *whop-whop-whop* of the blades. Just then, the door opens up on the right hand side of the bird, and two tan legs dangle out the side, with brown hiking shoes and tan laces dangling in the air. All three men are staring up, surprised at the activities in the sky just above their heads. A Ranger Boats cap flies off and into the water. Their hair is blowing in the draft of the aircraft.

The woman, previously with legs dangling, jumps the short distance from the helicopter into the front of the boat. Her long, brown ponytail blowing in the wind. She looks up and makes a 'thumbs up' hand gesture, and in two seconds the helicopter is up and away. In just five seconds it is eerily quiet.

The men stand with their eyes wide and their mouths even more agape. The woman breaks the silence, she speaks to the man in the back of the boat she's in. "I need to get in that boat." She gestures to the boat Jim and his assistant are in. But the other guy's feet seem stuck, like they're glued to the carpet. "Come on, let's toss a mooring line or...here, this'll work," she says, as she grabs a net from near her feet and passes it to the other boat. "Pull," she instructs.

The assistant in the front of Jim's Ranger Boat does as instructed, still confused by what is transpiring. It has been all of 20, maybe 30 seconds and everyone can hardly digest what's going on. A woman jumped from a helicopter into their fishing boat and is giving orders that she needs to get into the other boat? Crazy.

But then something clicks for Jim that he's met this lady before.

She knows exactly what she's doing.

Jim echoes the same order from the stern of his boat. "Pull!" He reaches his hand out toward the pro-fisherman and they pull the boats close together. As soon as they are aside one another, the girl hops into Jim's boat.

"Are you Justine? I've met you before, haven't I?" Jim scratches his head. "Are you the pilot that rescued Gus and Pops back in May?"

"Yes, you remember me," Justine answers. "Gus has been trying to reach you by phone and text message. You must be in a dead spot for cell coverage. We have to go, right now."

"What happened?" Jim asks, panic creeping into his voice. Jim's heart is suddenly in his throat. "Is it Annie? Or Pops?"

"It's your wife," Justine answers. "I just know from talking with Gus that Annie's at the hospital and we have to get you home A.S.A.P."

"Oh no. I shouldn't have come so far north. It will take us three-plus hours to drive back."

"Not for us it won't," Justine says. "How fast can this Ranger Boat go?"

"More than 60 miles per hour."

"Then let's get back to the cabin. Throttle down, Jim."

Jim starts the motor, and calls to the assistant in the front of the boat. "Hop over into the other boat. You guys can follow. We're in a hurry." The young man in the front jumps across as ordered, and shoves Jim's Ranger Boat away. Jim quickly stows his expensive camera into the hard-sided, foam-lined case. He snaps the latches shut and tucks it under his feet near the driver's console.

"Is everything okay?" Jim looks like he could throw up.

Justine knows scared when she sees it, and she's seeing it on Jim's face right now. "You get us to the dock, Mr. Roberts, and I'll get us down to the Twin Cities."

Jim musters himself together. "You got it. Hold on." And he throttles down on the big Ranger 620 with the 225 horsepower Mercury Opti-max on the back, the motor groans with sheer power. He kicks up a wake that rocks the other boat, but the other guys aren't far behind once their gear is stowed. Within seconds two Rangers are racing across Leech Lake at a breakneck speed. The afternoon sun glistens across the water. The light is golden, and the two boats are traveling so fast they are but a blur to anyone on the shoreline watching. *Whaaaaaaaa* the motors scream, each at their own pitch and slightly out of tune to one another. The other guy runs an Evinrude so they run with different sounds.

Justine is used to being the pilot in these kinds of situations, not the passenger. She's holding on to the 'oh crap' handle in front of her and on her left. But Jim's a good driver and quarter-cuts the waves. He's going so fast he's really up on top of most of the waves, making little steering adjustments which allow him to follow the pink-lined trail on his GPS unit—the route back home.

In about ten minutes Jim throttles back when he sees Pops' float plane tied up next to the dock, the same spot since the fishing opener. This morning it was on his mind that he'll have to find another place to store it with winter around the corner. Not sure where else to put it—who knows if Pops will fly it again. Now with this news of Annie in the hospital, it is the least of his worries. And then he remembers this pilot doesn't just fly helicopters. She flies planes, too. She brought Pops' plane back to this very spot this spring.

He slows the speed machine further as they approach the dock to their cabin. As he comes off plane the wake washes up and pushes the boat up and forward, but Jim's an expert at handling his boat. He's plenty far away from the dock so that the wake doesn't push him into the pilings. He slowly motors up to the front of the dock, adding reverse to dock gently.

"We'll use Pops' plane, won't we?" Jim asks Justine now that it's quiet. "Will you fly it back?"

"That was Gus' idea. If you're okay with it."

"Yes, let's go."

"We'll take care of putting your boat on the trailer, Jim," his assistant calls out, as he hops from one boat into the other.

"Don't worry Jim, just go," the pro-angler adds. "We'll take care of everything here."

"I'll trailer the boat back to your house," the assistant adds. "If you're okay with that."

"Yes, yes." Jim is a little flustered, but he remembers to toss the truck keys to him. "Lock up the cabin, make sure it's ready to be closed up." He and Justine start untying the mooring lines on the float plane.

"You got it."

Justine does her exterior pre-flight routine with even more care, knowing the craft has sat unused since May. She checks cables and pulleys, examines rivets, seams and fuel. Soon, they climb aboard the hot-musty airplane. After all the checks and continued pre-flight routine inside, the two begin their taxi away from the dock, with both boats safely off to the side.

The airplane's engine picks up in RPMs. Justine lets the craft warm up, engine building. "You buckled up?" She turns to her right to ask.

"Thank you for doing this, Justine," Jim replies. "Yes, let's go." She pulls the throttle and the engine revs to a screaming high pitch. With the forward movement, the pontoons on the bottom of the aircraft bounce clunkily across the wavy water. In a moment, the lake lets go of its pull on the craft and the wings sustain lift. Airborn. The fastest route back to the Twin Cities. But will it be fast enough?

Chapter 14

"I think you need to do it, Dad. It's worth a try." Gus is on the phone with his father, urging him to hurry.

"I'll ask Justine." He explains Gus' idea.

"I'm okay with it if you are, Mr. Roberts," Justine answers.

"Call me Jim, please."

"Okay, Jim. If you want to get closer to the hospital and save the extra time, I can do it—if ATC will allow it."

"Hold on," Jim speaks to Justine and gesture toward the phone. Then he puts the phone back up to his ear. "Gus, we're going to give it a try. We'll need a little help to know exactly where to be."

Jim listens with an occasional 'uh-huh' as he's tracking what Gus is saying. "Okay. Gotta go. Bye." He disconnects the phone and stows it in his pocket. Then turns his attention back to the pilot, Justine.

"Why would air traffic control not allow it? This is a float plane, and the Mississippi River is water to land on."

"Not quite that simple," Justine answers. "Post 9/11 that is."

"Oh, I hadn't thought of that."

"The metropolitan area around Minneapolis and St. Paul are controlled air space. We'll need permission to be that close to downtown."

"All that changed when planes flew into the World Trade Center, huh?"

"Yeah," Justine answers. "We'd be in trouble without permission. They take this kind of thing very seriously."

"Will they give us permission to land on the river? It's so close to the hospital, it will save me at least a half an hour or more of travel time," Jim says.

"I don't know. Gus had another great idea, glad he suggested it to you."

"Yeah, he's always thinking ahead that boy. Let's ask."

Justine fingers the com controls for the radio. "Area approach, this is One Niner Zulu," She releases the toggle on her radio control, and turns up the volume.

"One Niner Zulu, this is area approach, go ahead."

"Approach, I am a float plane in route to the Twin Cities from Leech Lake. Normally, I work out of Brainerd area with rotor. I have a passenger that needs to get to the University of Minnesota Children's Amplatz Hospital. We're up against a time clock here, folks. Requesting permission to land on the Mississippi River so we arrive right next to the facility."

"One Niner Zulu, that's reserved for rescue aircraft only—EMS."

Justine looks at Jim, but when she speaks into the radio there's no doubt she's communicating with her aviation peers. "Wish I had my Bell 300 right now. I'm an EMS helicopter pilot. Just a problem that I'm just in a fixed wing not a rotor. My usual heli-pad won't work for this craft. Perhaps there's a little leeway for extenuating circumstances?" Justine gives some pertinent information about her employment.

Silence.

"They're not saying anything, Justine."

"No Jim, but that's good news. If they were going to say no they would have just said it. The longer they wait to answer, the better our odds of getting a yes. They might be calling up to Brainerd to check me out."

Radio silence continues and Justine adjusts her path with the hopes that a yes is coming.

"One niner zulu, permission granted."

"They said yes." Jim and Justine high five.

Then through her com, "Thank you, Control." Justine adjusts some switches and changes direction with a bank turn. In a few moments she turns to Jim, com off. "Now...let's hope all goes well with this unusual landing."

"You can do it though, right Justine?"

Silence for a few seconds. "Let's hope there are no power lines in the way—or fishing boats out on the river," Justine answers. The last bit of daylight is slipping away quickly and some evening lights flicker on in parking lots and street lamps.

Jim nods his head and looks down at his cell phone as it vibrates. Incoming text message. Again. He's been staying in touch with Gus but every message sends more urgency that he needs to be there. He looks down at the dark purple modern-looking building with the unusual-shaped roof, lights just turning on. He opens his phone and sees a message that says from Annie, but he knows it is Gus with her phone.

It reads: *Dad, I'm at the shore. I see you. Look for my light."* Gus is using his mom's cell phone flashlight app and shines the light in a flashing motion.

Jim scans the darkening water and shoreline, looking for a flashing light. "There's Gus," Jim says as he points, thankful for the light. It's flashing long-long-short, short-short-long, short-short-short. Morse code. He'd never see him without that aid.

Justine drops altitude knowing exactly where she needs to be now. The Minneapolis skyline lumes large on their right. The tall buildings glisten with early evening lights, some colorful like a crown of jewels, perched on a king's head. St. Anthony Falls' movement is breathtaking. As they approach lower, the 10th avenue bridge's arch lights cast a pretty golden glow over the water. The Guthrie theatre has a crowd of people on the cantilevered deck. Several people point up at the plane now just a short distance above the river's dark surface. The new 35W bridge is right there.

Jim's stomach is in his throat for more than one reason.

"Looks all clear," Justine offers, scanning up and down to spot any fishermen or recreational boaters on the water.

"There are a couple of people casting from the shore." Squinting into the last light of day, Jim points in the direction of three guys.

"That's okay," Justine mumbles, as she continues scanning the surface. "No boats."

The plane banks hard and the view shifts to the trees with the changing tint of fall colors. But it only lasts a few seconds, and then Justine is coming back across the water for the landing.

"Here we go, Jim." Justine brings the plane down, ten feet…five feet…lower…then the pontoons connect with the water. The connection pulls the floats down, jarring Jim in his seat. Gravity grips quickly to slow down the plane. The engine screams, the pitch much louder on the water than it was in the air. Justine uses the pedals to steer the plane to the shoreline near Gus.

"Thanks, Justine," Jim says as he unbuckles his seatbelt and opens the cabin door. "I owe you big time."

"Just don't get mad that Gus charged all this to your credit card," Justine adds. "Seriously, though, I hope everything…and everyone is okay."

"We would pay you double what you charged us."

"Thanks Justine!" Gus calls as he peers around the door into the cockpit, standing next to his dad.

"Hi, Gus. Thanks for thinking of me to help with this one."

"If I ever need a rescue pilot, Justine—you're the one I'm going to call." Gus reaches inside the cockpit and opens up the glove box and pulls something out.

"Well I hope that doesn't ever need to happen again. Next time let's just get together for fun."

"Yeah," Jim exhales. "I gotta hurry."

Gus closes the door from standing on the outside pontoon, and jumps across to a log jutting out from the shoreline. It's getting dark now, and this is new territory, but luckily the quick-thinking planner grabbed the flashlight from the glove box in the plane. He hands the flashlight to his dad while he keeps the cell phone with the flashlight app. The guys look up—it is a long ways to travel—straight up.

"I'm comin' baby," Jim mutters as he sets off at a brisk pace.

But will baby girl Roberts wait for him?

Chapter 15

Even *In-Fisherman* magazine can't hold Gus' attention this evening. He tosses it down on the coffee table in the waiting area for the umpteenth time. The hospital lobby waiting room—a place he didn't think he'd be when he stepped off the school bus earlier. He inhales a deep breath and takes his time exhaling. Breathe. Good advice when stressed. Big. Deep. Breaths. His thoughts are prayers that everything is going well.

The cell phone in his pocket vibrates. His mom's phone. He looks at the caller I.D. His brother Jake.

"Hey." Gus answers it, and walks from the area with the fish on the wall to the front lobby where the windows and skylights look like bubbles.

"What's going on?" Jake asks.

Gus explains.

"Now?" Jake peels off a dozen questions without leaving room for his little brother to answer.

"The big purple building—University of Minnesota Amplatz Children's Hospital, Jake. Same as before. Dad just got here."

"What happened?" Jake asks, a little more urgently.

"I don't know Jake," Gus replies. "Should we tell Pops?" Gus looks at the revolving door just a few feet away. A giraffe toy rides 24-7 in the doorway. Perhaps he comforts young children that have to arrive to a hospital. Lots of little things in this place make it a little friendlier for kids. Right now, even he can't cheer this family up.

Gus clicks off the call and stows the phone back in his pocket. Maybe he should wander up to the fourth floor—Obstetrics. See if there's any news. He does. Just as the elevator doors open, his father is following a cart pushed by two nurses. Gus watches from a few steps behind his dad, surprised at the raised voices and stern sound coming from the hospital staff as they bark orders for people in the hallway to "make room."

They're moving fast. The silver-grey cart has a clear plastic tub on the top of it, and a little pink bundle is wrapped inside. Gus backs up to blend in with the wallpaper, wishing he were somewhere else.

Gus wants to form questions. Questions like: "Is that my baby sister? Is she okay?" But instead he watches with cotton mouth.

Jim is trying to stay with them. Gus looks hard at his dad and sees a frightened expression that just doesn't fit with this big strong man. Jim's always been able to handle anything. Gus stretches to match his stride. Staring into the cart, he sees a little pink cocoon of blanket. He looks closer and sees a couple of pale cheeks and the tip of a nose. His new little sister.

"We're headed to nick-you," Jim tells Gus while walking together. "The baby's in trouble and we're taking her down the hall."

"She's...she's in t-trouble?" Gus stutters. "Intensive Care...for babies?"

Then the group pushes the cart—an isolette—farther down the hall and behind double doors. As they close, Jim looks back at Gus and gestures for him to stop. Panic has settled on both their faces.

A lump moves up into Gus' throat. His hands shake. Gus' dad is a strong man, but right now he looks scared to death as he steps through the NICU doors. Gus has never seen him so shaken before. He needs a strength from somewhere else. On his own, he doesn't have enough. And neither does little baby girl Roberts.

The elevator drops and the doors open on the second floor. A bell dings. The sound jars Gus from his zombie zone. *What was he about to do? Where was he heading?* He steps forward as the doors begin to close, and he walks slowly down the hall. His eyes don't seem to focus, everything's a little blurry around the edges.

Left foot. Right foot. Odd how the body just does its job. He isn't thinking about walking, yet his feet know what to do. He follows them until they stop in front of a beautiful spot. Chapel, a brass plate labels the entrance. He pulls open a strong wooden door with etched glass set amidst sand-colored marble tiles.

He steps forward, his mind and heart already praying. To his right he sees a framed piece of art from the St. John's Bible on the wall. Comforting. He's seen that before. Then, straight ahead, he sees a series of paths that entwine in circular motions cut into the wood floor. The path is a different shade. His brain fast forwards, looking for the word. *Labyrinth*. Without thinking or even realizing it, his feet move him forward. There's definitely an entrance to a labyrinth—his feet know what to do, where to go. Left. Right. Stay in the path of different-colored wood. He prays, just talking to God as his feet move through the pattern, the turns and curves comfortable with a slow and steady pace. Not really going somewhere, but definitely on a journey. He prays about his mom, his newborn baby sister, the doctors and nurses, his dad, his brother, even Pops. And when he gets to the center of the labyrinth, he just stands and listens. It comes to him: *Be still and know that I am God.*

Gus thinks about how fragile and tiny the baby is, and how his Mom's heart would break into a thousand pieces if this baby died. All of their hearts would. He cries. He slumps down onto the wooden floor on his knees, his head buried into his jeans. Hands folded above his head, tears catch on his long-sleeved t-shirt.

He stays that way for quite awhile.

"Are you okay?" the voice is gentle, and a hand on Gus' back has a light touch.

Gus lifts his head and uses the sleeve of his shirt to wipe his wet face. He nods. He notices some pretty jewelry on her, and a cleric's white collar.

"Do you want to talk?" The lady has a warm, husky voice. And a nice smile. "I'm a chaplain here," she says with a smile. "I can leave you alone if you're okay. I just wanted to check." Her voice is inviting.

Gus takes a deep breath. He tries to speak but his voice quivers.

"It's okay, take your time." She sits down on the floor next to him, a gentle hand on his shoulder.

Gus clears his throat. "My new baby sister just got rushed to the NICU.

I don't know if she's going to be okay or not – or even if my mom is okay or not."

"Wow, a lot is going on in your world." That gentle voice.

"I haven't even met her, but I want her to be okay."

"Of course you love her. She's a new treasure."

Gus nods.

"There's a story I like in the book of Matthew. It's about an exquisite pearl. Once you find it, you'll do anything to keep it. Even if you didn't know it existed before, in a heartbeat it becomes your treasure."

"Yeah. I didn't really even see her. They were just hurrying her into the NICU."

"We have a world-class NICU here. I'm sure they will do everything they can for her."

Silence.

"What's her name—do you know?" the chaplain asks.

"We haven't named her yet. Not that I know of, anyway. Things have been kind of discombobulated tonight. That's something Pops would say, he's my mom's dad. He has a way of talking that takes a little getting used to."

"Pops sounds like an interesting guy. Where is he? Can I get him for you?"

"He's at the V.A. hospital. Recuperating from a stroke while we were at the State Fair."

"Oh dear," the chaplain replies. "You have had a lot going on."

"Yeah."

"What's your name? I'll just pray for her as your little sister."

"Gus."

"Gus' treasure, like a pearl," the chaplain-lady replies.

Gus thinks about the story from the chaplain about finding the most exquisite pearl and selling all you have for it. "Ma'am, I've been saving up money all summer for something special. Really special, and really important. But I'd give all that up if this baby and my mom would be okay."

"Oh, Gus. That's so sweet. But it doesn't work that way, does it?"

"No." Gus shakes his head, looking down. "And I know it doesn't. But I think I understand the story about selling all you have to keep your treasure now."

The two talk for awhile longer about the family and getting Dad back quickly from Leech Lake. They pray together. Gus is glad for the company with his prayers, and he tells her.

"Where two or three are gathered," she replies with a smile.

The door of the chapel loudly bangs open. "GUS?!" Jake runs in, hair askew and red-faced. "They sent me for you." He huffs through his words.

Gus hops up from the floor and wipes his face one more time with his sleeve. He takes two steps towards the chapel door, then stops and turns back. "You need help up?" Gus asks the chaplain.

"Yes, thank you," she replies while down on her haunches. "Bad knees."

Gus walks back, and she takes his offered assistance to rise up from the wood floor. "Thank you," she says.

"Thank you, too," Gus answers. "For talking and all."

With a small hand gesture that could hardly be called a wave, Gus sets off down the hallway to the elevator with Jake. He watches his brother hit the call button with an arrow pointing up. But are things looking up two floors above? Or have they been summoned for a different reason.

Chapter 16

"Boys," Annie calls out when the two sons walk into her room. "Come here." She extends her arms out for a hug.

This is the first time Gus has seen his mom since having the baby. And, the first time since he found her on the floor in the house. She looks tired, her long shiny black hair tied back in a messy bun.

"How are you?" Gus asks.

"I'm okay," Annie replies. "She came a little early."

"Is…is…she okay?" She, Gus wonders. The little pink bundle in the clear plastic isolette.

"That's why I wanted you here."

Silence. It lasts an eternity.

"Dab nabbit, Annie. Spit it out." Pops pipes up from sitting in the corner of the room. Gus turns quickly, not realizing he was there.

"Pops!" Gus calls out. "What are you doing here?"

"I made Jakey bring me, that's what." Pops' speech is a little slow. "Now Annie-girl, tell us what's going on. We're all here."

Annie takes a deep breath. "She's tiny; just under five pounds. And she needed some medical attention," Annie answers. "Dad's with her now. I'm so glad he was here in time."

"Where is Dad?" Jake asks.

"He's down at NICU," Annie answers. "That's why I wanted you all here with me."

The two boys look at each other, lost for words.

"Just sit with me and keep me company. I'm a little worried, I need my guys with me, it'll help keep me calm." Annie pats the foot of the bed and Gus sits down on the corner. Jake pulls a chair up close.

"What happened to you, Mom?" Gus asks. "Were you passed out or something? Earlier, I mean. At home."

"My blood pressure dropped, I guess," Annie answers, sounding tired. "I'm glad you came home when you did, Gus. And really glad you helped get word to Dad to get him home. That was some pretty fast thinking."

Gus shrugs his shoulders.

"It was, Gus," Annie continues driving her point home, patting him on the knee. "You organized the pilot and helicopter and using Pops' plane. You even thought of landing on the river from what Dad told me. You helped stay connected with my cell phone and found a spot along the river bank. All that brought Dad straight here. That saved a lot of time—and we needed it for the baby."

"Have you named her?" Jake asks.

"No, actually. We haven't," Annie answers. "I thought you two were going to come up with a couple ideas to choose from."

"I thought of Louise," answered Jake, looking over at Pops. "After Grandma." He turns back to Annie.

"Oh, that's so sweet, Jake. My mom was amazing and I miss her so much." Annie chokes up for a second, thinking about her mother that died when Gus was born. Everyone's quiet, emotions are high. "Pops, what would you think if we named the baby Louise?"

Pops just nods, and gives a crooked smile.

"Cecil Owen mentioned everyone called her Weezer at the baseball game," Gus answers. "I like that nickname a lot, Mom."

"Did you come up with anything, Gus?"

Gus looks down at his hands. "Well, I have a little bit of an unusual idea. I'm not sure I like it better than Weezer, though."

"What is it?" Annie asks.

"Well, at first I thought about CeCe, or Cecelia. That idea came from Mr. Owen. But then I heard this story from a chaplain tonight in the chapel downstairs," Gus continues. "About how a man found the most amazing pearl, and after finding it sold everything he had to keep it."

"I know that story, it is beautiful story of faith," Annie answers.

"So I was kind of thinking I liked that better," Gus continues.

"What?" Jake asks. "I didn't hear a name in any of that. I don't know what you're talking about."

"I think I do," Annie replies, thoughtfully. "Tell him, Gus."

Gus stalls. "I kinda like Weezer, Mom."

"And I kind of like your story and the name that you picked, too," Annie prompts. "Tell Jake what it is."

"Pearl."

"Oh, I get it," Jake jumps in. "Baby is new in our lives, but already she's precious?"

"Yeah, like that," Gus answers. "We've all been pretty worried about her, and I don't really even know her yet. I'd give every dollar I have in the bank for fishing tournaments if that would help her be healthy."

"Oh, that's so sweet, Gus." Annie reaches out and hugs Gus, then extends her other arm toward Jake and brings him in to the three-way. She's quiet for a minute.

"Pearl Louise—I like it." Annie smiles, recovering from the sadness. "Let's hope and pray little Pearl Louise is doing better with all the high-tech care in the NICU."

Just then the door to the room opens up and in walks Jim. But he isn't alone. Will this nurse along with Dad have good news or bad news about this new baby sister with a pretty new name?

Chapter 17

Jim is a big man and nearly blocks the entire doorway. But as soon as he steps aside there is a nurse with a pink bundle in her arms.

"Do you want to hold her?" Jim asks.

"Oh…" Annie holds out her arms. The nurse brings the baby over and places her in them. "She's so beautiful." She traces a finger on her cheek and across her nose and forehead. Tears of joy well up in Annie as she opens up the blanket and kisses the tiny little feet. The baby girl is sleeping. Content. Tiny. Looking healthy.

"Is she doing okay?" Gus asks.

"She is," Jim answers, and sits on the edge of the bed, nestled up close to Annie and the baby.

"We'll keep her in NICU for tonight," says the nurse as she steps back to the door. "But everything has stabilized so it seemed a good idea to have a few minutes together. Good for everybody. I'll be back."

"Let the boys hold her," Annie says to Jim, passing the bundle.

Jim stands and places the baby in Gus' arms. For a moment a look of panic crosses his face. And then he realizes she won't jump like a fish and squirm out of his arms. It's pretty easy holding a baby, especially a newborn. He relaxes a bit and takes a good long look at her face.

"She looks just like you, Mom."

Annie chuckles. "She looks just like you two boys."

"Hey, how'd I get left out of this equation?" Jim chides.

"Strong Asian genetics, Jimbo," Pops replies, half-smiling.

"I guess," Jim answers, as he picks up the bundle from Gus and shares her with Jake.

Time drifts away with pleasant talk and the occasional accent of baby squeeks and coos.

"Pearl Louise, eh?" Jim repeats after Annie tells him their idea. "I like it. You like it, too, Pops?" Jim brings the little bundle down closer for Pops to see her. He nods.

"I think I understand about my name a little better now," Gus brings up quietly.

"Cornelius Gustav," Annie offers to him, formally. "I hope so. We weren't trying to do anything that hurt you. Cornelius was a famous ancestor and Grandma Weezer's father's name. And Gustav was Pops' dad's name. So we just pulled a little family heritage into yours."

"I see that now," Gus replies. "Maybe it isn't so bad after all."

"Really?" Jim asks. "You'll use it? Cornelius?"

"Well…I don't know if 'use it' fits," Gus replies. "But I won't be afraid of it anymore. It can be on my fishing license and my hunting license…and one day my driver's license," as he looks over at Jake. "Or on my school records. I will just deal with it."

Jim and Annie exchange a look, and then look down at the little baby in Annie's arms.

"Look how much you helped your big brother already, Pearl Louise," Annie whispers, but everyone can hear. They all chuckle.

The door opens and in walks the nurse. "I should get her back and you should rest."

Annie holds the bundle up to the nurse. "May I feed her next?"

"Sure. Give me an hour and I'll bring her back to you," the nurse replies. "Meanwhile, take a rest. It's been a long night." She walks out with the baby and the room is quiet.

"We'll let you rest and be back in the morning," Jim replies.

"It already is morning," Annie replies. "4:30 in the morning." But she yawns and as the lights are dimmed in the room. She nestles comfortably into the covers. Tired, but happy.

The guys back out of the room, wheeling Pops in his wheelchair, and close the door. For a moment they stand in the hallway outside her room, not sure which direction to go, or what to do. They leisurely walk down the hallway. Jake pushes Pops.

"4:30, eh?" Gus replies, looking at his watch. "It's Saturday morning, Dad. Everyone's getting up for the tournament in South Dakota today. Having breakfast. Gassing up the boat."

"Yeah," Jim rustles Gus' black shiny hair, and thinks for a minute. "How about we all head over there next month for a little pheasant hunting?"

"That would be great." Gus' face lights up like a Christmas tree,

"I think wrestling practice will be in full swing by then, Dad. I can't go this year. But you three can," Jake offers.

"Not gimpin' from a blasted chair. I can't hunt this year," Pops harrumphs. "Maybe next year."

"Walleye fishing on Waubay in the morning," Jim adds another idea. "And pheasant hunting in the afternoons."

Gus thinks of the new gift he got a week ago for his birthday, the Beretta Silver Pigeon. "That would be a great weekend, Dad. Let's do it, even if it isn't the tournament that I was saving up for all summer."

"About that, Gus. I have another idea." They walk down the hallway together. "There's a two-day team tournament next weekend on Lake Minnetonka I wanted to tell you about. And the entry fee is…"

More Journal Notes...by Gus Roberts

Let's Get to the Bottom of This!

Fish often like to settle right at the bottom of the lake or river. Why? There are at least three reasons why that I know. Maybe you know more reasons.

First, fish like to hide in structure. It makes them feel safe to have stuff all around them. Bigger, predator fish might not find them, or even if they spot them, the smaller fish can often be safe tucked in close. It's instinct. They're just trying to stay alive. Structure can be rocks, weeds or logs along the bottom, or can be changes in the bottom's shape, like a drop off or a shelf.

Second, there is often good food along the bottom. That's the other part of a fish's goal when the new day starts: stay alive and eat. When food is there, the fish will follow.

Third, water temperature. When the water temperature is warm near the surface, fish like cooler temps farther below the surface. The surface temperatures change a lot in the year. Lots of fish just hunker down on the bottom.

Here are some good ways to get to the bottom of things:

1. Sinkers or Weights   You can add these on to your line to get your hook down. Some pinch on (also called split shot) and others thread through your line like egg-shaped or walking. You might want to use a snap swivel to attach it. I like the no-snag type that keep you pulling through the weeds.

Slip Shot   Egg-Shape   Barrel   Walking   No-Snag

2. Jigs   Get heavier with your lead-head jigs to get them to drop down. Jigs come in lots of sizes so move heavier -- from 1/16 ounce to 1/8 ounce or 1/4 ounce or 3/8 ounce or even 1/2 ounce. Be sure to feel for the jig to hit the bottom. You'll feel it. Then reel in to bring it just above the bottom.

The more current or the more wind, the heavier jig you will need to get to the bottom.

3. Bottom Bouncers   I really like how bottom bouncers keep you in contact with the bottom. They are easy to fish with because you can really feel it keeping contact with the bottom but your lure stays just above the bottom. That's where you want to be so the fish strike.

Have fun and catch some nice fish!

The adventures of Gus Roberts continue
in the Fish On Kids Books Series.
Read them all.

Discounts available for schools. Re-seller opportunities
for bookstores, gift shops, sporting good retail
or non-profit groups looking to raise money.
Contact us at:

Fish On Kids Books LLC
PO Box 3
Crystal Bay MN 55323-0003
email: info@fishonkidsbooks.com
website: www.fishonkidsbooks.com